True

To life,

Michael Melin

True

— A Last Book —

Notes from Journeys
By Foot and Bicycle
in South Dakota in
Spring and Summer
1987

Michael Melius

with illustrations by Ross Burden

TENSLEEP PUBLICATIONS
Aberdeen, South Dakota

For all my English teachers, but one
Seriously, for those who dig the wells, and mind the windmills

ISBN 0-937603-10-4 paper; 0-937603-11-2 cloth
Library of Congress Catalog Number 91-52925
Printed in the United States

The illustrations on pages 6 and 44 are by the author.

Suggested Chapters

(Second thoughts. The book about the book. Should you doubt or wonder at anything here, check the notes, where it may be explained.)

writ slow to be read slow

These are the days we've nothing to do
and make everything up

This book is urged on by my apprehension that our landscape and time, and the very feeling of how it is to be alive here and now, go unnoticed and unrecorded and in time are forgotten. As they change and the people who remember them pass, neither the landscape nor the feeling can be recovered. This may be true of any age, but in ours the changes are on a scale that makes the forgetting profound. Change, forgetting, change, on and on until we can't remember or imagine how our lives could be otherwise.

This book is about slowing the changes, noticing, and never forgetting. About recording it is of two minds, at least, for it has the contradictory purpose of driving you away from books. It will fail if you keep reading.

—When not-forgetting *means* recording, faithful and true. It means good writing, so the words disappear, live to die in bearing ideas. The book is a container for ideas, now open.

Noticing involves all the senses, is more than conscious.

Slowing the changes means the ideas become actions, including no-action.

The urgency comes from thinking how profound those changes are. It seems that the earth I love is being erased by and for people who don't remember, if they ever knew, what it is they are erasing. Their forgetting cooperates with the erasure: no one notices. Their lives get farther away until there is no turning back. They learn to like it. The earth that gave their riches meaning is gone to provide those riches.

My part, then, was to be absorbed by the earth so that I might speak for it, it might be remembered, loved, and the changes slowed. . . . And in doing so I might learn: to what extent is life on earth travail and ordeal? And of what is left, what part is joy?

I do this for the earth, for myself, for you. For myself because I am one of you. As close to the earth as I do live, it is I who need to notice, to remember, and to change.

To be setting out. Your first steps close a door behind you and you're gone.

I wanted to be one who set out, became so turned to the earth I never quite came back. I was seen passing through the land. To give myself wholly over to the earth, forget the connections with the "real world"—even "July" will no longer exist....

To place yourself outside, receiving. To be that body, touched. To break the schedule and go, if only for a minute's standing in the rain.

I wished to leave all that behind, now, before my landscape and time were further changed. To be no more a part of the forgetting, the change. After all, the change was in the nature of a change in thinking, distancing myself from the earth and forgetting it. Having come so far in this direction, going back now meant taking a great leap. No retracing steps, no gradual adjustments or acclimation, no shortcuts, no cheating.

To leap, throw your hands away and follow. To step, fall forward and catch yourself in time. Stride is fluent, as these parts merge in coordination.

By the simple measure of walking the earth I would surrender to its requirements and its possibilities, relearning them from the ground up. True to the earth in speaking for it. And let the thoughts take the shape of the land. Impressed. A rolling pattern transfer, snug on the earth, transcribing a spectral landscape. Or a sensitive recorder, set in earth's idiom and obliged to translate the mute-for-unheard songs. An attempt to catch what passes and underline what doesn't, realizing that the fleeting and the permanent are both soon forgotten.

Pause where a rock appears from the steady grass, then step over it. The grass good fuel, the sun good light, the mind a lens for burning.

Only slightly, or so, is this the tale of *my* mind. It happens to be mine. It will come up. You will require some background information. But only as another aspect of the tale of a mind in a body set down on a planet. The planet, body, and mind speaking through me the writer who is neutral. It is the one with the words, that is all, and might like to read them, too, someday:

With these words I stand in celebration and inquisition of the place and time in which I was raised.

I want to be awake for this
and step outside

March 19: The beginning is a problem, for I set out the day before a predicted blizzard—no one will believe I could be so daring, or so dumb.

I walk and walk before I realize my ears are straining—for what? Before I think, I know: spring. The ears come forward to confirm what the other senses already know, in new light, clouds rising from the ground, and the earth releasing waters I never thought it had. It is the water's sound, and the liquid songs of returning birds I lean into the wind to hear.

What my feet have already observed, as mud. My boots have collected a rich pastel of soils, mostly from a brief, dumb foray into badlands gumbo. But it is heavy, wet, and on me so only briefly aesthetic.

Earlier it was jumping cactus my feet collected. It is one way to map the land, by what your boots compile: the cacti were on private land, the badlands are public. I could have predicted it from a conventional map.

⨀

A side-creek camp, junipers and elm trees for fellowship and fire, coyotes for crazed accompaniment. Twists of grass to sit on, to brush the boots, to throw on the fire and see.

outside the poem never ends

March 20: Misty rainy all day, and the wind rising. The old story: a blizzard coming.

Down to the river, the river Cheyenne, where eagles define the mist with their dark appearance.

Evening is the mist blackening, darkest to the west. I pitched my tent amidst trees by the bluff and prepared to accommodate the worst as it arrived: rain, driven rain, driven snow, night. I set fire to a log jam left high by some other spring. After that, not much. An ordeal. Turn circles by the fire, basting and roasting. And it wasn't that long of an ordeal, somewhere short of heroic. I retired early, the blizzard eight hours old and already signaling its end, as they all do, by being quieter longer, simply quieter longer. Sometime in the night the silence woke me.

ears leaning into the wind fall forward when it's not

March 21: The west side of every tree is plastered with snow.

That cloud, that blizzard, obscures the rising sun awhile before giving it a drenched blue sky to shine through. The sky to the south is whitened by light reflecting off snow. There is snow everywhere I'm headed. I'm suddenly concerned with going snowblind.

The sunshine state: a zigzag path is prescribed. West, then east by afternoon. To see better, and longer. But the river's deep valley offers little choice for direction, and will force me to face south unless I trouble to rise out of it. The river's pattern looks like this, viewed from above:

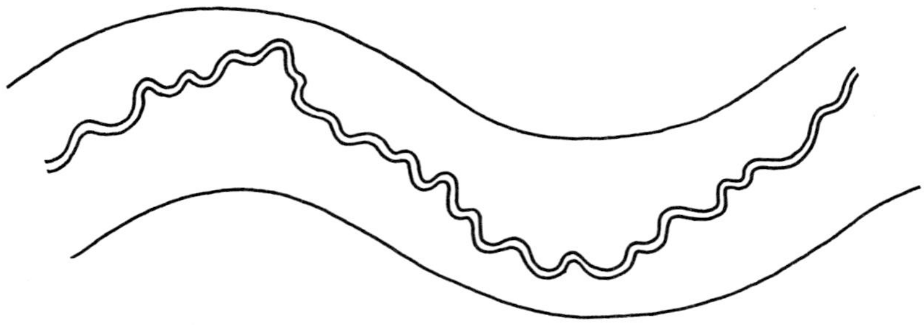

And below?

I packed my goods and climbed out of the valley to the west, a steep rise to the edge then abruptly flat above. In last night's wind this edge was the first rest that some of the snow enjoyed. First and final rest. It lies here in great drifts, soft and deep. I stopped—but what is stopping?—and exhilarated myself by running and jumping off the edge into the snow. A not uncommon dance of the open country, and the *best* way to release the blue light in snow. The leap is everything: faith, freedom, flight, release, return.

Returning to earth. "The rising sun" is not only false, it is small, suggesting a limited vision and sense of place. To be confined there all your life— Breaking out of this earthbound view, contrarily, entails strapping the earth to your back for a good long while and taking a look around. Repose. The sun is central, but you may turn away and see other stars.

O

They matter so, the sentences we construct about the world (this one is about the world's sentences). A sentence could start or lead anywhere, and the world offers few clues, not even nouns, for where that should be. Even "world" takes a limited stand. We want the most all-embracing noun possible. And for the nouns of lesser embrace— river, tree, snow: to connect them true, so thoughts match the world.

March 22: I have become a bluebird net. As I walk I am straining a certain volume of air for their blues, their song, their river of migration I walk into. With experience my net tightens and extends. I miss little. As I walk I can gauge their river's current: in streaks perhaps, or following the Cheyenne; in fine or foul weather; at night.

And meadowlarks—they will have to come up sooner or later or this account will simply be untrue. For yellow. You can stare at the sun only so long. I suggest you let a meadowlark reflect it for you.

O

The snow is not melting fast, in that way snow has of preserving itself. The snow takes all the light offered, then lets most of it go, producing a uniformly white landscape in which only the hardest shadows can display. Yet sometimes it seems the air's own riffles are revealed as faint shadow motions on the snow. If not shadows, starpointed *beams* catch your eye on the snow. They are spectral, and flash the colors over your eyes when you move, as each point flies past. Or you may stay, and let the sun, with the snow as its lens, pass the colors over your point of view. *But where is the point? And who stands in the way of these beams?*

My feet are better grounded and think the snow is drudgery. So I welcome the slightest deer trail. One I find is well-worn by many deer, but as I walk with it it forks, and thins: I am leaving the place where they met.

Mid-day rest in a sunny dry spot on the shore. The river's surface bears life, rounding the bend and floating past: mergansers, oblivious to me seated stone-like. Whether to move or stay? Whether one experiences a truer version of the world in motion or by staying put. In motion there might be *more* experience, but of a fractured world, of beings in recoil from your motion, and you unable to hear over the sound of your own moving. The other a stone's view of the world—sentient stone—entered long enough and the sparrows come to light on your shoulder.

○

Barren areas of the prairie—rocky, poor soils or trampled areas—appear from the snow first. They caught less snow, which melts fast on the dark surface. The waters pour off, and it stays barren. And so it is, or appears, that tall grass grows where snow catches where tall grass grows.

Land-use along the river seems all of a piece also. (I've just come a dreary mile, the river in the mind of one particular owner.) Willow islands inundated by cockleburs and mud, with no fences paralleling the river to restrict cattle. The floodplain overgrazed, barely supporting grasses that should thrive only in drier situations. The cottonwoods cleared to grow hay. Large trees felled and only the smallest branches cut for firewood. Living trees used as fenceposts. What fences there are, are down, the barbed wire left snarling anywhere. Junkpiles in the side draws, junked cars set along the riverbank to stabilize it, awhile, before slicing their way downstream. But they won't persist, can't out-tumble the river stones, and will be reduced in time to iron sand.

It doesn't last. By evening I found an eagle's nest in a lone cottonwood by a riverbend. Increased every year, the nest by its size could be my age. Nobody home, and the eagles around here seem northbound. A great body of air, eagle air, is gliding north, leaving a good, a mild winter along the river. By summer these will be vultures, as vulture air displaces eagle air—it could mean something to someone, to those with eyes at the tops of their heads.

March 23: The day north-windy and clear, I float south. Crossing the flats above the river, irrigated fields: no details. No obstacles. I walk with my eyes closed, saving them for other sights.

Late in the afternoon I passed an owl, asleep, day-roosting low in a tree. I approached from behind, from down the deafening wind, and was quite close in front of him before he heard me, opening his eyes wide. He looked shocked, I think; but I never saw his face again, I never knew him well.

I heard him later, at night. In one of the bleaker settings I'd been, and wishing for company, I wondered what strength will last us through another day, who or what will draw us home if we weaken and fail.

O

the days I can't open my eyes wide enough
the nights when closing them doesn't help

March 24: The river and I turn west. What part of a river flows uphill? The valley.

Somewhere in the gray afternoon I climbed a ways up the steep north bank of the river for a rest and a view. There were places bare of snow on the black, sun-facing shale. As I sat there a coyote came up the valley, aiming to cross my path at right-angles. But she stopped abruptly at my tracks and sniffed: my presence to her seemed as certain as a wall is to me. Then she leapt through it and bounded up the slope beside me, even faster as she sensed me near, out of sight as far as I could see.

There was a moment today, emerging from the trees onto a terrace north of the river, with the river curving around and the valley spelled out before me, south to north: juniper, cottonwoods, sage, yucca. All softened by falling snow. Add my tired feet, and that I know just how far it is to the ground, and can crumple in one motion: you really must reach those places of beauty in such dimension that you cannot decide which direction to turn.

March 25: One of my boots fails me and has me limping. I'm looking for a road, a ride, a town, repairs, recuperation. I found them all and more: from the people in town reacting to the sight of me, backpack, gaiters, and getup of the outdoors type. One and all commented first about the weather I'd been through. Of these there were two sorts. Most common were those who shuddered at the thought that seeing me provoked. The others knew what I'd been through and looked at me sideways, inspecting. I think they were being kind, for despite thinking me a little crazy they tried gently reminding me that it can get *nasty* out there.

The first group tried my patience immediately, or at least after my initial astonishment at their consistent reaction—there were three or four in one hour. I started to mutter, "you get used to it." Or, "you keep moving." Because these were the very ones least affected by the weather, living from house to car to work to car— Granted that the difference between becalmed sunshine and driven snow is *definite* for both of us. But I had been out in it and didn't think it was so bad.

I definitely have to get my humor and patience back to communicate with these people. They are the ones I am trying to reach through this journey, such a journey, and the accounts of such a journey, this journey. It appears I will be meeting as many people on foot as I will through these pages.

○

I really believe this: If you make heaven of the sunny days the rainy ones won't be such hell.

Make heaven of rain.

March 31: Today I am finally out there, blown by the wind and taking my course and instructions from the land. The land has become silvery, bright with melting snow and the water running off. It is hard to get around, with mud and all the little streams to cross. But it is the one time of year we have such adventures—daring stream crossings, and the possibility of getting ankle to head soaking wet: an exciting time to be alive.

Spring. The *sound* of water. A half-mile away, calling. Our little creek, with rapids. Unrecognizable. *Our little creek?* Walking along with the sound I could believe this is the way it is, here, all year. My pace quickens. But I know better, and actually it is the rarity of that sound, of the water with force, falling, that draws me to it every spring: it will not last. A week, at most. Little room.

if every spring was the same, if they never ended

Where the rapids are the stream narrows and produces the sound, and there is the leaping crossing. I like this knowledge that passes from experience into the body, lodged there to emerge later when needed again in experience. The way I circled this little butte, knowing without needing to say or think it that *this side* would be out of the wind, the place to set my tent. Just coming here, without fuss or show, the body's habits of thought allowing the mind to wander.

April 1: Then the wind switches 90°, hard from the north, and flattens my tent at midnight, with me in it.

And I am a straw man in a wayward world. There must be a way to describe today. If words could roll, and toss you. Clouded in convolutions. Boisterous, yelling, then calm. Sudden rays of light. The day ending in deep reverent night.

○

to live from moon to moon, and know exactly what night this is

Each spring is new, once and only. And each is the same, advancing north by degrees, with a first day, the day the air and all the elements take more from the night than they give. But the earth and snow hoard the night well, and the sun is a while that first morning in piercing the moon-glazed surfaces. The day breaks into the thinnest places first, up the windblown hill; the snow there is a lens that burns itself. At first it is a change so subtle as to be imperceptible—some melting and puddling—so the first day of run-off is usually not recognized until the second day, in retrospect. It was the day of pause, the day of wait, and how could you have missed it? Because now it is too late. From here the days accelerate, with no looking back, and the morning of the second day is prelude to the afternoon, and that *sound.*

Earth holds the cold well, so the surface melts and slips away before the base has begun to thaw. Hillsides warm in the sun, the barren and south-facing first, and right away the little draw is ahead of the big down stream. (The sheet the rille the draw the creek.) The streambed is full of snow, and when the waters from above meet the snow they turn it to slush—plain dark slush, advancing as a stain, saturated and oozing. One can walk right up to it over the snow. The slush front. Its progress in a place is once and only, followed as it is by the tumbling stream that first flows over the slush then down through it. And its progress with the year—north with the sun and east with the streams—is once and only. We do well to follow it.

Water and snow. The one time of year these are brought together for us: in the pure snowy field with the creek just starting a line down the center, silvery white like the sky you'll see when there's water to reflect it. Intimate, the earth and sky, and these days the one becomes visible: shades-of-blue haze.

Flooding and fog. The easy back-and-forth of ground and cloud, of hilltops steaming in the sun, each with its own cloud, and cloud shadow.

In the evening, when the flooding meets the fog—is it really *fog* or the cold sunset air sweeping west and *lighting up* the air's water as it comes?

Now as the night settles in—and there should be a young moon—the cold reclaims the earth and all the elements again, the thin and still waters first, uphill, held back from the creek that rushes on, dark water—the wind is right and I can still hear it. By morning it will be trickling again.

○

A rush of air from the night sky, the sound of wind: wings, many wings: a flock of ducks. Right over this place I've chosen to rest.

the many places   under wings

<u>April 2:</u> Wings and other unnamed sounds, croaks and whistles, flying by in the night: the season cannot stop reminding me of itself, long into the night, *is* a spring night.

Spring is a complete time. Each element suggests the others, and to feel one is to be convinced of all the others. The high and warmer sun, silvered earth, fragrant air, more sound than silence—the very light is becoming inarguably spring, bright through the haze.

○

Water always makes perfect splashes. It doesn't take long sitting beside a river before I can think, "the water isn't moving."

○

Only three weeks ago I was wondering, "how can there be so much silence?" The answer was winter, or night, or both at once. The question was posed by the silent land and sky. In the sunshine since the question has grown to: how can there be so many voices? Now is the time to notice this change, while the differences are so striking, before these birdsongs become routine. We do get used to silent winter. I'll get used to this throaty spring. This year I may even keep up with it.

The season would just as soon rush ahead without me. I've rarely let it. Sometimes I wish I would, or could. The season is and is like a rising river I can't rest beside. I may go with it or against it but either way it's rising. "Too late now!" the river taunts. I'd do well to craft a boat. I can see leaves tumbling along beside me in the stream, and I'm keeping pace, but I don't dare stop. There are many crossings ahead, days and nights, until I wonder what difference it makes which side of the stream I'm on. How can both be home? And all the while I want so much to dally in the rabbit-run plum thickets.

At this date night still freezes the rivers and lets me catch up. So mornings are the time for making progress, for getting ahead of the river before the surface turns to slop and we dream of boats again.

—As the flooding reaches a peak. All the stock ponds are overflowing, easily. Below some the ground is settled with little fishes, bluegills of the bluest blue, iridescence on the black ground. Left by an afternoon's surge, they mark the water's broadest course, a sort of comet's tail, strand and stranded until rescued by some redheaded flock of ducks—

the many places without wings

April 26: Spring resounds with every muscle, there are no thoughts of escape. I set out again, past familiar flowered hills to where new ground awaits me like a blank page: wandering allowed.

A dry April. Growth before rain, in hesitancy and haste. Leaves curl back as the flowers unfold. The day? *Fragraria.* One wants to walk, to breathe, and sample the air, here, there. Especially for the surprises, invisible clouds one stumbles through: phlox carried down to me from the hilltop, cottonwood in bloom, and clover, I declare, growing. As if we breathed because the earth is sweet.

○

By dusk I am seated overlooking badlands to the north. A pronghorn crosses the flat way behind me. After a while I look again to see it coming towards me. I half turn to watch it: cautious, sniffing, step by step towards me until a hundred yards away it stops and *something changes* or happens because the antelope snorts and stomps and goes away. But not too fast.

April 27: Each time I set out I am soon overwhelmed with a feeling of freedom. It enters through the skin, or the lungs, reaching the feet before the brain has a chance to doubt it. The feeling that the future could be anything for me, direction or pace, as much or as little in each day as I care to take or give.

As free as I am dumb. For there is no easy way through, no strolling over this ground, soft old hills of shale furrowed deeply by the years so that even the way of water is not easy or welcoming: steep-sided, curvaceous, muddy. The mud, the curves, their steep slippery sides—I go that way. The average molecule, reaching the river by mid-day.

Again the Cheyenne, but then we've hardly exhausted our acquaintance. It seems to open the earth to view, inviting us in for a sense of its construction. It looks small for its valley, underfit, as if it is a trickle of its former self. As if it might someday return. At any rate the valley cuts through former valleys, ancient Cheyennes—these old, old, Hills. It is outwash from the Hills, it is ice jammed and bulldozing along, and rocks riding downstream on the ice. It is a south wind. It is a cottonwood forest, a cavity nester's dream. It is dammed upstream. —Always, in transcribing the landscape, of what goes where and how and next—it is a human landscape, touched sometimes most profoundly by a hand most unseen. So in describing any place such as this river one must not assume *this* is how the river is until one has looked for the hand: the cottonwood forest exists by dint of the suppression of scouring floods and fires and even beavers. And then? More bluebirds? More beavers?

○

To evening on the shore, my little rice-cooking fire is *over there* now, this warm evening. Also new is the color in the northern sky, reflected in its river. Long into dusk I see a raccoon exploring the shoreline, silhouetted against the water.

April 28: Morning climbing up and out, above the river to a sharp pinnacled ridge between two tributaries, looking down on two herons flying north.

The day? *Spiniferus.* First while climbing junipers and snooping into old magpie nests for owls, broken-branched swinging out of control—but for this hard sternum I might be carrying a piece of juniper around with me, the walking wood sampler. By mid-day walking bare-legged through last year's cordgrass, not yet reduced by snow and rain and rot but in all parts sloughing off bit by bit to a dry point. One way to grow skin like leather. And in the hot afternoon by the river, playing with a spiny soft-shell turtle, he groggy in waking to his hibernation's long morning.

○

I find that in crossing the land as in crossing a page the only way to get somewhere is to start, just pour forth and soon enough obstacles, which are meanings, appear and only the right words will lead you past them. The page left blank is the place not unseen but worse, seen without comprehension.

Imagine me traveling all this way without stories to tell, connections to make, and observations and comments for all time. Nothing came of it. Unimaginable, not to say impossible, that something notable, even timeless, wouldn't happen. I'm setting out to see what might be found here, dreading that it might be less than it was, and less than it could be.

As a result of a banal process—walking or writing—pattern, meaning, and significance appear. It is the thing to do, to be out in the world, making sentences with a language that extends, not limits, your understanding of the world. Mostly you want it delicious, *feathered to the toes.* To be brought right to this moment, intense snap! freedom, choosing return, to a body perched on some meadowlark's point: it is a human, singing of these things.

○

between gusts of wind, the gusts of birdsong

So many of the open-country birds have *expansive* courtship flights and calls. As if they had the whole sky and were bound to use it all. The ducks airborne show nothing fancy, just straight-out winging, tried by strength and endurance. But the others seem unbounded, flying in spiral columns, skyrocket bursts, or great arcs and undulations, and always with exuberance, or exaggeration: the harrier's heart-stopping rolls, the hawks' paired free falls, the short-eared owl's applause, the curlew's long waves, and the horned lark, petite but with a courtship flight that is a spiraling and binding of the air with wings and song.

○

Evening where Sage Creek pushes into the river, an enchanted forest of cottonwood and juniper. It seems to go on without end in the falling night, magnificent junipers encircling cottonwoods whole. They appear to make a perfect duet, meant for each other. Why they are paired like this here and no other place I've been is a mystery.

April 29-30: Through the Badlands, strictly by the valleys.

The day began in more sweetness, dew and sunrise and junipers. A morning that was all the mornings ever in its sweetness and light. Tree shadows arrayed, suspended in the haze but failing to preserve it. For morning gave way to another white-hot day. I was going to explain how April is the August side of March by saying, "April is the cool August." Maybe next year.

○

Sage Creek is: turtle tracks and shale landslides near the mouth, grouse dusting beneath the junipers, owls young and old, hawks and shrikes, pronghorn badger porcupine deer. Racer vole and viper. And bison bison bison. They have a way of appearing. From out of a ravine, from behind a badlands flute, one bison immediately dominates the scene, big and black and wild and suddenly there on the same plain as me. At the last water (I assumed) before the top of Sage Creek valley I stopped to drink and swim, eat and rest. A bunch of bison came up to me, sniffing, moving towards me as a group behind daring leaders. They stopped finally about twenty yards away. Lined up cheek by jowl they look all head. They seem unable to stand next to each other for long before the slightest move from one starts another a-throwing its head, inciting the first, and the two square off, butting and snorting.

I didn't know what to do, or how much closer I should let them get before I—did what? Whether to raise their ire by moving or wait for it to develop anyway over my seated form. Not that I had much say in what they decided to do. With only a scrawny cottonwood I'd shaded by, and nothing to climb but this sheer 60^0 knife-edged ridge in front of me, I had terrible choices for escape. But I'd climb that steep wall if I had to, and live.

I couldn't wait and they wouldn't go away so I talked to them, said I was going over to the pond for a drink. There I could at least swim away and if they came after me I'd grab one and ride him in the water. They let me go, turned, throwing a few punches with the motion (guard your flanks), and browsed away. Always posing.

○

I wonder about buffalo wallows, places where the bison roll and kick up dust to ward off insects. Mightn't they perpetuate themselves in a cycle of wallows holding water breeding insects biting bison kicking dirt? —Without attributing intelligence or purpose to a hole in the ground.

○

Hunkered down along these dry washes, with my little cooking fire, my drab dusty clothes and dark dusty skin, always makes me feel so *aboriginal.* As I've often seen them pictured. I hope I have the same alive, intense gaze, and then look away.

I did walk to the farthest reaches of Sage Creek, to where the clouds divide, to the peaks separating Sage and Cain Creeks. (There are two sides to these badlands.) Near the top the grass is left in pedestaled patches, and only a few of only the spiniest herbs remain, or have invaded. Barren. The image everyone has of the Badlands: hot and dry and blasted by sun and wind. But they are that no more than the country surrounding, so what sets them apart must be the soil, if you can call it that. In a matter of a few raindrops it changes from dust dry to wet to sealed and shedding water. Then it goes back to dry as readily when rain is done. It makes poor soil for plants, first choking salty wet then sunbleached bright and dry. The sun from all directions, as if we needed more. It is made of volcanic ash and deposits from ancient lake and river valleys, marshes and deltas. They seem to be reluctant sediments, not given to a life on land but ready to return to the sea, to make the rivers run white, to deposit themselves in the Gulf. Perhaps to do it all again someday.

To go to the top then is to rise but higher through these strata, what's left of them; it is to ascend to the rarest of the strata. —Unremarkable, but crucial here, where that one layer is a hardened rock ledge that preserves its position in protecting the softer layers below. The always-slanted, often-steep badlands go level. What is more, other layers of steep badlands remain atop the ledge: one can walk freely among the pinnacles.

To the north the slope is gradual, even imperceptible, with natural arenas formed among the peaks as the ledges are preserved in steps, concentric arcs around the low place where the water escapes. To the south the ledge had cut off abruptly and was left two hundred nearly vertical feet above the valley. So this is the Badlands wall. The view to the south obstructed only by air. The wind this day was a clear, bright, gorgeous south wind, strong at this height. Overhead, swifts floated in behind the pinnacles and up into the wind, were thrown back to do it again.

It was the wind that made it, and the view, and the ledge, set among the pinnacles. No, it was the view that made it, and the ledge. . . I am trying to keep this subdued, restrain myself so you will believe me when I tell you of its magnificence. Perhaps you will appreciate by how often I've since regretted leaving so soon—as often as I've vowed to return. But I was nearly out of water, with a perilous, steep descent of the south face between me and a pond I could see below; I had to go.

Who gains these places earns them, but may not stay to keep.

The descent was hell, two feet down for every one out, but it is done, forgotten until needed the next time. *Who weighs the effort when the effort is past?* It was soon replaced by the singular excitement of being at a spot just seen from above, that spot brought close, then others, leading among the network of ravines to the pond. But I'd have missed it on my left had a killdeer not called from there.

The pond is blue on earth, cool blue sky reflection. The blue through eyes fulfills the mind's image of water so completely the whole body knows it; we'll soon drink. There's a teal, a grebe, a rail, and the red ribbon of a garter snake flickering amid the waves. Around us all the while two pronghorns pant, a buck chasing a doe. Round and round, near and far, they do go on. Keeps the heart strong, I suppose—and only the strongest.

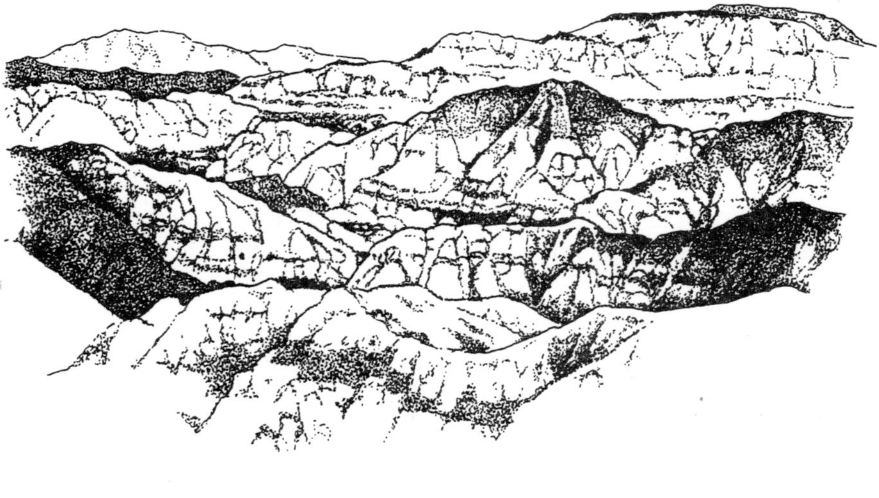

May 1: Into Interior by drunken ride with two hippy Indian biker types from who knows where. I pick up my too-small box of food at the post office and talk to people about where I'm going next—through the rez. One old guy tells me to put a stone under my lip to put up with thirst; he learned it in the infantry. He looks World War I but he means II. He's buying whiskey, feeding his cold.

To the White River and across, my Friday break in the shade. (Move like an hourhand at the base of a cottonwood.) Bathe and do laundry. (Just walk in the river, lie down, roll around. Enjoy. Scrub with sand the dirty spots, or moor yourself and passively wave, letting time in a river wash you clean.)

The river is too white to drink from so by evening headed upstream I was thirsty again and stopped at a ranch for water. It is an idyllic setting, beneath a ridge, between the river with all its trees and the broad outwash plain of a tributary. The owner was looking over a corral with a bull and horses and seemed not at all surprised to see me. He took me to his shed where he had a jug of ice water on the back of his tractor—he freezes it every night for the next day's work.

We talked of real things, the Cheyenne and White Rivers and the differences, the land between, and how the tributaries had flowed this spring—trickles, but with rain forecast for the weekend. Then all at once he faced me squarely and asked, "Do you ever have much to do with the Bible?"

"Uh, well, yeah. I read it now and then."

"Did you know that the Bible says. . ." he quoted from memory. And then again. Seems he'd recently found Jesus, and had "accepted Jesus' blood in his life." He could see I hadn't, and was about to save me, the pilgrim come to his well.

I can hold my own and even manage to enjoy talking with people such as him for a while, and can quote a few myself ("many will come from east and west. . ."). And there's always the chance I could convert him with just the right words—it's a fair game, once joined. But before long my eyes start to roll, my attention wanders, I'm nodding and saying 'hmmm' to everything he says: the withering monologue.

He was adamant, insisting that nothing we do in this life has any meaning or significance to anything or anyone, even the Lord, except as it serves and pleases the Lord. Only what we do for Jesus has any meaning in the world and to Jesus. He is grim, and thinks pygmies in the forest are as doomed as I even though they haven't heard the word, or *warning*: I gather he'd been scared out of whatever wits he had one night while sitting around a campfire in the Hills, listening to tales of hell, the ultimate kind where you burn forever. His faith, that is, was motivated by fear.

I put up with it long enough to earn more water, made some conciliatory sounds and promised to think about what he'd said—then got permission to camp that night on his land by the river.

○

Walking the ridge above his place, on the slope where the ridge breaks and falls toward the river, I found a patch of Easter daisies. Next to a plowed field. Now I'll have to tell him how precious these are, on any scale of space or time. Then the thought occurs: How much would I exchange with him for a promise to preserve these plants? How much of my soul. Odd reckoning, but possible. Could we trade canons?

The thought sets my head afire. I am infuriated with his conclusion that none of this matters, except as it gets us in or out of heaven or hell. Not that I don't agree. But his thinking stops where mine begins: knowing that nothing need be done, we begin to move. It is terrible, true, that nothing matters, and everything's relative. It seems like no place to begin. It stops one. But it is the only place, the place everyone, to be true, begins. Nothing need be done. The very emptiness of the beginning gives weight and meaning to the next, the first step.

I am infuriated with myself that I can offer him no sure alternative for direction or purpose, for what to live for. Earth? The stars? These plants? I have no proof that there are no sins against the Lord, nor that there are sins against the earth, but only sins against ourselves.

It's not fair, his acceptance on faith—or fear—of what I cannot see. And what I can see he rejects offhand. He put in a good word for the earth, to soothe me, but even then "God made it beautiful for us." He would have people give themselves to Jesus. I would have them return to earth. He's upset I won't be saved today, or ever. I'm mad at his damned frozen water. I wonder if there are days he has to wait for it to melt before he can drink.

His religion could embrace mine, were he willing, by celebrating and preserving earth as an act of love to God. It won't happen as long as his plans include only himself and God—mirror god that blesses whatever he does in the name of God. (The rest is setting.)

In my obsession with him I almost forget all those who have no god, who renounce even that little of an imaginary guidance. Who reject hell (and give up heaven in the bargain) to be free of responsibility; who have no alternative in our culture, no ultimate purpose or future to lure or threaten them into or out of any act. Who bless themselves. Who play God. Who would accept not believing in anything in order not to believe me, in order to avoid the question altogether.

And then no one asks what are we doing here. No one answers, rather. We ask, and recoil, for the question seems to open up a great empty space for answers. Find one to fill it, quickly: heaven, family, country. Humanity? (Our team.) We'd accept an answer on faith and leave it at that rather than face the question again. Meanwhile, the prospect of an unlivable world—the one we're supposed to live in to become saved—is our very real situation, and we'd do ourselves a disservice if we didn't wonder how we got here.

Localities we've made unlivable before, but this prospect of an unlivable world is new, as is the necessity of going beyond the personal to see the self as part of a larger system, and its actions there ultimately circling round to affect the self in the future. Until choices and actions are made not just for personal reasons but for ecological ones as well. Or they're made first for ecological reasons, the ecological as personal. There's difficulty in achieving that level of connection, understanding, and responsibility. And it would be so much easier not to care, to discount the ecological self and leave reckoning for the spiritual self. I wouldn't know.

That evening as I walked the hills above his place I saw one of the biggest rattlesnakes I'd ever seen, near his road. I left it alone, I always do, but this time there was some satisfaction in thinking I was leaving it to him. *Give us this day our daily snake.*

in a dry country
thought sweetens rain

May 3: Down by the river trying to outlast the rain. The river brown by now, and rising, I would imagine. But I would imagine everything from inside my tent.

The second day of rain. There's no end to May.

The first minutes of rain were the sweetest, as you know. That fragrance rising from earth is life itself, life and the promise of more. I hadn't anticipated when I set out that I would be such a *breathing* thing, and heartily, for these sweetnesses go right to the blood. Lately I could believe they are what moves it, and what moves the legs.

What moves the earth. For I have been a tired thing, and seen myself walking as rolling the earth at my feet. Surely this is true. And such a heavy world it is. My heels burn. Imagine doing this with the hands.

But whatever for? Why roll the planet from here to there? Certainly the air need not be pursued. Yet I have seen it, the air appearing there: the golden mists of a hillside steaming in the sun; the cold air later flowing down that hill and unrolling as fog; in the dust from hooves, smoke from fire, our winter breathing. And these to me I would again return.

But it's to the air invisible I turn now, to clouds of plum and phlox and clover. The clouds of surprise. For unlike the mice we are not noses foremost, but eyes, and always surprised when the world mixes so directly with the brain without consulting the eyes. Then the eyes are swung until the flowers are found, and the earth is rolled to bring them closer.

But *I* haven't moved.

These flowers have taken the air and the other elements and distilled them to these fragrances, for whom I don't know. I have no designs on them, good smells or bad I roll them through me and about me and carry them on a ways. A cloud of my own swirling behind me.

(The animals who've smelled me: deer and pronghorn, bison and badger. The coyote.)

So with little regret the wood ducks and I are holed up in the rain. There will be much blooming beyond this. I suppose I could go on about the wonder and meaning of rain, confusing the viewpoints of earth and rain and me: roots swelling, the earth floating its cracks filling the earth sinking—puddles. But for now I'm in a tent imagining that in days to come I'll find ground so slick it will roll away from me, I'll grab it with all fours—

rain
darkens the dead
brightens the living

May 4: Morning still raining I crawl out and wade over to a neighbor's place, amazed as I learn that I chose the only high place around for my tent when the rain began two days ago.

This is all I require: the view from above the clouds, time-lapsed satellite image of this great cloud spiraling away to leave us in the clear. If not I'll want to consider the neighbor's offer of a barn, tempting if only for being classic, traditional travel: to stay in a farmer's barn. Or I could make excuses for hitchhiking home, like a rainscape is news and I should explore it on familiar ground, where I have a memory to compare it with. But the spacecraft shows that the clouds will depart this day, and I head south through the reservation.

The White River curves around the Pine Ridge and one creek after another drains the land—the clouds—between them. Atop and between the valleys is undulating sandy prairie and farmland. The valley sides and tributaries are steep clayey badlands, while the valley floors are fairly level and grassy but much insinuated by gullies. The effect is extremes side by side: steep by level, eroded by lush. Water dripping everywhere.

I believe I am seeing the badlands in their true form and color, which is mud. More or less dried mud. In-the-making. Slow but episodic, here now it's speeded up so the process becomes visible. Two days of rain have exposed all surfaces new to the air and the eyes: fresh, washed, never-before-seen strata appear, each ancient layer's first light.

Out of the valley to the west I rise. By the time I reach the top the rain has ended and the waters stopped flowing through the grass. Already I miss them. But the landscape I tread this day is distinguished by impermanence. I missed a splendid photograph because I sat and watched instead of running for my camera: when the clouds were first tearing apart and beams of light were traveling up the valley and highlighting, but softly, the far other side—with the clouds still dark and low it seemed that the light rose from the earth itself.

Moments such as this, of unadorned beauty in undiminished clarity and joy—such moments will always occur. They are not absolute but relative to time and place and person, and therefore unpredictable. This moment was born in the promise of sunlight displayed on green grass, a moment more precious for being impermanent.

It is essential to expose your heart to the world and let the two fall in love, wed, become one. Hurt for the places gone. May your heart never again be so rent. May the hurting for the lost places prepare you to love their being, and inspire you to protect the places remaining. But you'll not know hurting until you know love.

May 5: Secret.

Secret. You thought perhaps I was going to tell you everything?

The rain, then a clear cold night: the badlands in fog. Stark raving landscape cloaked in the most caressing of weathers. With morning comes mistfall: the other valley, air, falls through the clay valley, whose pinnacles emerge from the fog as floating castles.

I am off this morning to the west, the sandy sage and yucca prairie. Along a slight road I walk past a group of 1940s-era cars left in a circle. There a coyote is coming towards me, catching grasshoppers. I park myself and watch. Wise, she walks upwind; they fly down. Sometimes she catches them in mid-air but most she pounces on when they land. The coyote turned up the old road and towards me, the stone antelope. She sees me but keeps coming, looking. The curious dog eats, I suppose. But then she turned aside before the cars and played on, eating.

O

I don't get far. At a certain point with the creek spread glorious before me I say to heck with traveling and settle in to learn one place well.

No matter how slowly we go we tear at the fabric of the world that's developing without us. We tear, pulling shreds behind us, thinking they are unattached to anything—they tear so easily—only to come later across some hole in the fabric: our effects have preceded us.

The world that runs away from me, before I even know it is there.

To make barely a wave, then; to *be*, wholly and exquisitely, in the world without interrupting, much less overwhelming. To only cast shadow.

Or what like waves runs away from me may never return. Learning to go, or stay, without ripping at the fabric. So the tear may be benign, mending in a blur of absorption; you in its self, absorbed. Try knowing how you're received. Until you go so slowly you blend in, out standing but not outstanding.

If to blunder through a place is to rip a path then to live there is to *be* a path. Another pathway of energy. To do so intelligently, so as not to be just another wave in the blur of overlapping population curves—such intelligence takes time. To realize that "harvesting this will subtract from something we ultimately want more of, flower, seed, or womb; how can we sustain ourselves here without exhausting that which sustains us?"

Walking I've been eating the fruits of pincushion cacti that I chance upon. They are tiny but bright red on an earth brown and green. And eating them helps me see them; eating red, seeing red. I could swallow the many black seeds within and they'd go that route. But I prefer to spit them out as I walk on, in hopes there will be more when next I return. Imagine all that it means that I scattered some thousand seeds beyond where they could otherwise have gone.

If to live in a place is to be a path then living nomadic means learning a succession of places that connect. It requires harvesting from each without depleting, and connecting the places, the springs and sheltering woods, with strands of food plants. Asparagus, I'd suggest, and plums. Learning to store food, in fat and cache. Learning to go hungry.

<u>May 6:</u> It's a muddy May. Do you know where your beef is?

I flushed two meadowlarks from their nests, each with five eggs. The snakes eat well.

The plum clouds are restored, and rising to the sun. There are lovely springs dripping with ivy

(secret)

and the stream curling out forever in shade, in sunlight, an out-and-out maze deeply cut into badlands, truly wearying never ending until I crossed, guessing at a side stream: I hope my pack is at the top, the very top, under the first tree. The maze all over again, uphill. More secrets.

But this place is starting to get to me. It seems tainted, or spoiled. Perfect, but with an overriding flaw not immediately visible. Beautiful but dead. Heavenly, without souls. Not just for my being alone; that's the story wherever I go. But today I finally notice there are no tracks. Of deer and pronghorn, that is; coons and coyotes and rabbits I've seen, but the three days since rain should have left many hoofprints to read—a confusion of them, on the road, by the springs, in all this mud.

I've seen only two deer and one pronghorn the whole time, but it is the absence of tracks that awakens me, eerily confirming what the other senses have recorded:

Everyone knows what happens to the deer tracks. I'd been told, I'd been told, and now I'd seen it for myself.

It makes me realize how often I'm looking down, how much *ground* I've seen in my life, and how often there are tracks. Years of walking inevitably reveal rules about the land, and one is that only the most wasted place is without tracks. That this place is flourishing, undergrazed (if there is such a thing), and that there should be many deer; that they are rare: it confuses my senses, tormenting my mind.

Is the scene repeated in valleys across the reservation? The game all hunted out, prairie dogs poisoned, the land leased or sold to white folks to graze or plow? And all this glorious country without the grace of a person walking through it.

All the sentences I construct to explain it begin with "Indians. . ." They emanate from a place of pain, that wants to be done with them. I hope to set them forth in innocence, in asking your help in revising them.

How is it the natives of this place seem to be going dead wrong? Could it be they feel no moments of marriage, no hurt or loss? They whose spirit I thought was like mine, intermingled with the earth's, and to heal one was to heal the other. Because if the truth was told it would reveal that some of the ideals I pursue are to be found in their Lakota tradition: a serenity, an ease in the world that is acceptance and humility; the demonstrated ability to live without need, with meager means; demonstrated nomadism; their culture of sharing. "Indian time."

And I should add: land still preserved, unbroken and unspoiled. Land set for returning to, for remembering, and inspiring. Lands held in trust, set for habitation and rehabilitation, and may one not suffer for the other.

Saving land stops time. In this age especially, when our connection to our past is severed as the connections between the places are severed, thoughtlessly. Erased, forgotten, erased.

If not, then why don't we make our way through the plowed fields? Because going by the old ways we would have to skirt the lifeless plowing. There is no way, there. And how did it get to be this way, great areas of the earth where there is no way to go? How shall we recover those places?

Spreading seeds as we go.
Patching the earth by hand.
Taking the fences down from around the elk and bison.
If you plant grass it sings.

My first memory of Indians—real, not storied—was while traveling west from home, beyond the river, five years old and riding with my family in the car when dad pointed out a dark figure walking along the road. We kids gawked as we passed—our first Indian.

Walking.

My thoughts then were probably a giggly mix of fascination and fear, as much as I knew about the Sioux used to place that one. But at least we weren't on different planets anymore. From there it slowly gets better, my education by TV and movies and a couple paragraphs in the history books balanced by real encounters, local history, current events—impossible to be in South Dakota in 1973 and not think hard about the Sioux. It was a slow education, as much by luck as by intention and curiosity, in a state that should require native studies in schools, if any state should. Education at some distance, the distance not all by choice, so it can be said that I don't know what I'm talking about, or the context of Sioux history and modern experience, or just how it feels to be Sioux.

All true. But learning all I don't know about being a Native American has meant becoming white, and I'm not sure if I know how that feels, either. To see myself as a member of some race—European or somewhere in that area. When I could think that we are closer, today, as Plains people, than either of us is to our ancestors. We are natives of the Great Plains, with no desire or need to call any other place home, modern people but with a practical and spiritual need to connect with this place in person and through history. To know, for instance, that the weather will always be *so*—March the snowblind moon. The European heritage for all it has can't offer this, a deep connection to this region. We see the same stars as they do—and that isn't trivial—but they can't tell us how to live here.

And there is something evasive or disingenuous about reaching to one's grandfathers for credit or blame for how we are today. When eventually if not already we, too, are accountable. We who must now do the work of restoration, and drawing back. We have seen how we kill. We know it well. What might we be like, letting live?

If you are Indian then I am *wasicu* and it makes me forget that I come from another place where we are just people, born into the world as it is given and obliged to make do with what is left. The names keep us in place, secure but imprisoned. "People" is at least a larger prison.

And there are times when I could think that I am as native as any Indian I've met, for all my time on my feet in the sun, smelling the air and drinking the waters, really living with the earth and learning its ways. Isn't this a truer measure than lineage of one's nativeness? Yet my connection to the past of this place will never be complete. So it is from this position, not being home in either culture yet needing to reach to yours for that connection, that I am able to say: I need your spirit strong. I need to know what will heal it. Your spirit like mine.

May 7: I am saying this to the people who know it, throughout this book.

It's just that, yours is the direction I would have us go: attachment to place, humility, the earth restored and sacred. I could do worse than dream these dreams. How are they so blocked off from both of us?

○

I come out of the valley hungry this morning. My last meal yesterday was a pan of rice and vegetables. With five miles to go to the road I'm drinking water for power, serious about finding food. I came across two puffballs, plucked one, and filled my stomach. Nothing tasted better. —I've kicked many a ripe ball in the wind and have earned this one.

Onto the road walking the afternoon I'm begging a ride south, squeezing shade from a stop sign, trying to stay awake. All the stories I won't tell about the people I traveled with, but this one: I caught a ride with two farmers, one who enjoyed telling stories—about cattle rustled out of these creeks, of deer shot and butchered and only the quarters taken and sold, of white traveling fools like me beaten by Indians. I can't tell how much is story-telling, how much he's trying to scare me, or how much is sincerity. But I like the thought that when I was exposing my heart to the world back there I was also exposing it to bullets. It's fair.

I won't be scared off. Some other reasoning will have to come along to keep me away. It's the old story, white man sneaking through Indian country for some gold—to publish—

○

Into Martin and rendezvous with my box of food. Patient, now, holding it in my hand, I can wait, and enjoy this hunger awhile longer before I lose its meaning. Then into a grocery store and come out holding an apple. Just one will fill me. Grace with every bite.

This hunger, this freedom is available to everyone. No one is rendered so helpless by modern or dominant culture that they can't experience it. —It's a measure of how far we come that such statements seem ludicrous, and we can't recognize them as possible. We've inflated our wants so far beyond need we can't remember what having those needs feels like, and what fulfilling them means. No hunger, no grace. Meaning begun in humility, having water to drink.

May 8: Except now I'm in a cemetery south of Martin thinking the car just passing on the dirt road has stopped, will find me pack and maps and all scattered and profane. But I shan't sleep in this or any cemetery tonight. The hillside across the way is swept clear of mosquitoes by the wind, warm southwest wind fragrant with sand, abrading sage, abrading yucca. Lizard sand, whiptail sand, it-is-written sand. A new language to learn. (What is it about sand that suggests scales, and armor?)

I am listening to one of the most beautiful sounds I have ever heard. It's like a chorus singing a high, wordless song, rippling through the wind. Sweet confusion, hearing voices in a cemetery at night: I can't tell if it's angels or birds, and for a while I let myself believe in angels. I know it is a bird. I know that well enough. I want angels.

May 9: All last night the snipe flew over me, pendulous, winnowing, back and forth, rising and falling the sound in his fluttering wings. All night he went on, yes all night. The lowly snipe become angel.

○

It's evening again, where I'm waiting for the box turtle to come out of its hole. Or go in, more likely: its track is fresh, handstitched along the sides of the body's furrow, and leads into the sand. The turtle diurnal. Is it the only rock in this sand? Is it sand that polishes the turtle?

They say this sand blew down from the mountains to the west long ago. There must have been some golden skies then. The winds by now have calmed in inverse proportion to the rains, and the sand is more or less stabilized. In standing waves it shows a fossil print of the wind's lower surface as it was centuries ago.

Sand is its own best metaphor, so imagine a pile of sand spread out over your yard. Let the wind move it around, and water it now and then: watch the way the rains flow through these hills unimpeded. Hillcrests dry first, but being lower doesn't give much advantage by being wetter—it's just later in drying out. North-facing sand stays wetter, also, but that's a given in our hemisphere for any surface. Eventually the water reaches a less-permeable layer and starts moving sideways. And then when these hills ooze, they pour: where the water really springs it does so at a gallop, a river running right from its source. The layer where the water seeps shows itself a bright green, to me and all the visually prepared. It's an intense contrast of lush-amid-dry, as if someone instead of painting the hills green had poured all the paint out in a thin dark line.

Waterfalls again, along the spring-fed creek I followed into the hills. At the low falls (all of two feet high) I came upon a bull snake trying to go up the falls. I was wide-eyed, elated, appalled: this diamond gold and red thing tossed about in the water, falling back only to try again, persisting, but eventually going on land.

How to find the ornate box turtle? Get close. The earth itself is ornate.

<u>May 10:</u> Awoke before sunrise and raised my head and spooked three pronghorns coming down the draw, sniffing me out. Horned silhouettes on the dawn they stood stomping and snorting not thirty yards away, easing towards me and soon dancing off to the south.

I spent a good part of the morning playing with lizards. They are new to me. When they see me they fly over the sand, and I see them, as they run from yucca to yucca for refuge. Then my slow approach is meant to relax everything, but the air tightens anyway and then snap! they bolt again. My next approach is even slower, hypnotic—the hot sun—until my big eyes and their pinpoint of star are an arm's length apart. Then I can see they are half tail, striped yellow and green like the yucca. They climb around in it looking at me.

Where will I find shade! in these rounded hills. In my head? If I get desperate I could dig out a cave for it—my head—under a northside yucca. It was big news today when a cloud passed over the sun for a few minutes around noon.

By mid-afternoon I found shade in a lake. But not much shade. This lake you could swim across—half a mile—and wade back. There are clouds and storms all about and the lake makes them twice. With birds in and around the lake, I settle in with a splash.

I believe I have strayed over into Nebraska, by this lake not showing on my maps. So that's what the stone obelisk back there was, the red stone with 96m chipped into it. Even though the border here in our little pile of sand is as inapt as any, I have to draw the line somewhere, and shall reel back to the northeast from here.

○

The mind could not live without the senses but sometimes does best without them, and in its darkness goes where the senses cannot. I have the urge to dive into this ground and burrow through it, easy as swimming. Something about the sand, augering my toes into it, a smooth and soft and lightness almost liquid.

Too much peering into lizards' lairs. Or maybe it's just the pre-eminence, here, of pocket gophers. Because I imagine myself at home in the ground, secure and cool. Like the gopher feeling with its whole body me the beast tromping by on the surface. Not waking for it.

Think of soil as the thing least likely to have an idea of itself. But no, it heaves and hatches and hums with life, has rivers of air, seasons of warmth and cold, knows towards the light and away. . .You have to get down to mineral level before it stops. Or does it? Just now we wonder, what is alive? Think of all this glass sand ringing and trembling to the sun and moon.

This would be the sense to have, of the earth's most subtle fields.

○

The storms promised all afternoon are overhead, shriveling gracefully, and offer not even electricity. But they have shaded the sun long enough that when it returns it will be most welcome.

May 11: Coyotes every night, save last.

Snake and I don't meet: where's the design?

I resolve to bathe, eat locally, shade by cottonwood, and scatter eraser dust in every major watershed in this state.

This is the quietest, loneliest place I've been so far. No motors or roads, not many birds or even jets. Even the fences have a way of disappearing among the speckled hills.

From a postcard: It's a sad cycle that keeps everyone in their homes and me out here alone, and I'm relishing it. There aren't all those *others* appearing on the hillside over there. Sad: I'd like to share it. Instead I get what's left while they gnaw away at it (we're talking grass, meat, wheat, profits, sacrilege). Chew it good.

If I could surround someone it would be with this, white now pink now blue bouquet of clouds, hilled and green and freckled earth: sunset. If everyone could just pause, then everything possible stop. Come grand sunset or drab. —My hopes for a world gone wrong. If 'world' is the word for it. 'People' perhaps. Heck for all I know the world's going right. I've been out of touch for 2½ weeks; certainly some inertia has shifted my way? If inertia is the word for it. Sigh. I cannot speak to them but from here.

Here we have an ocean in sand. Waves, but slowly, in an epoch's winds. Now blow the winds west, now blow they south: the land lies in augered pockets or in crossing waves, canceled here, amplified there. Today was the first *very windy* day, and in a few places the sand reached my eyes. But only in places, for roots have loved this easy sand, and hold it, their leaves only sharpened by its blowing. This dry year the wind is gaining. . .

<u>May 12:</u> Another hilly day.

I don't get far. Too windy to travel, too nice a spot, my trip cut short. My ambitious twelve-miles-a-day plans reshaped by reality. I'll stay in each place longer, and hitch rides between places. —This occurs to me here, with uniformity for miles, one place like the next, the folly of travel. If exploration in detail can be extended by the imagination I shouldn't lose too much by the compromise.

Such a day: to be hugging the ground and flying with the clouds. Each one's arrival is cause for celebration, for a sky not sunny all day. Now and then a choice round one comes by and I stand to watch its shadow sweep towards me over the land.

How to scale the sky and clouds down to backyard size, imaginable. So they aren't just words, 'cloud' or 'wind'. This mass of air that today flattens me is itself flat-topped. Something races across, something wetter rises, cools, condenses, appears. Dissolves. The cloud bottoms stretch ahead while their tops curl up and over into dry air. From the clouds' viewpoint this wind is sweeping them from the sky. I take their side in the matter.

<u>May 13:</u> Moonlit walks. I should have to tell you about moonlit walks.

Last night I went looking for the kangaroo rats where their burrows must be. I found none, but did see a silver blinking eye in one of the holes. This morning the wind is done and there are new trails to follow. If I could learn to recognize the tail-marks for one of them I could follow it and relive its quietest moments, its greatest leaps. . . .

By afternoon I am down in a cool meadow wet by a windmill—someday I shall have to sing praise to windmills. The curlews concur. I am trying to catch the tune of the switchgrass. (Back on top the yucca makes a sharp, yes, cutting sound.) Sprinkle the hilltops with yucca, affirm the valleys with sod.

I had forgotten the lack of stones here until I saw some, white rocks collected in the bottom of a pocket. But they were bones, fragments so long in swirling in that bowl they were rounded to balls.

I have found four skulls, cows and others, and they were all upside down. I wonder who does this? Or is it four of a kind in a game of chance? In any case I've always turned them over, to make mouse hotels, to let the poor dead animal look at the sky.

○

the rules of eating:

gather locally
eat it raw
chew it good
shit uphill
think all over

○

It is *nice* being able to choose this life, to step into and out of it. An appendage, merely, of my sedentary, modern self. That is, not wholly nomadic, with no other choice: living root, berry, and sinew on the land. Scraping the bone bare. Adapting by hunger to the world, ultimately a hobo: nomads without the supporting culture.

But a culture centered around a nomadic life would make it possible, and less of a toil than this solo effort. So many of our systems, actions and articles would have been designed for it. But the culture doesn't support nomadics, so there's all this fabulous world being ignored, forgotten, erased.

So, burn. Burn the car, burn the culture, and go. Start again. As if creating a new language, and in the process learning about meaning and relationship and sound. But recreating the nomad, from the ground up. *It's a world we have here.* Everything applies. Adapting to whatever is given, be that shelter or flight. Not fighting it. Even the hunter eases into the life of the prey, to cut its trail, its vein.

My halting, cheating attempts at nomadism suggest at least the possibility, and an aesthetics, for such a path. Life in motion, a succession of places that connect. Needing less for having little for carrying only so much. Living lightly on the earth, encamped and free.

We are able, here and now, to take this path, at least towards living lightly. We have the freedom from want that makes the physical freedom possible. But we don't *go*, even voluntarily or occasionally. We've forgotten how, or even that we can. We've surrendered this freedom, and lost the ability or capacity to spend a day without work, without eating. We need to be reminded these are possible. We stand in contrast to those among us who have to know days without work or food: those who have to know both, we who never do.

○

A succession of generations, that connect. For what good are the traditions without the lives they sustained? Recreating those lives begins with a footfall, and leads to the old stories appearing by necessity. *Lost ones will reappear.*

○

Walking we'd be reaching for the seedheads of grasses for food, and the ones we can reach will be the first to go. We'd be selecting if only a little for those that grow too short to gather without bending, and improving their chances for replication in the next generation.

It takes such intelligence. Stupidity is rarely rewarded, only by chance, which works equally in all directions. So wouldn't things arrange themselves in the direction of intelligence?

Intelligence may be an end in itself. I've certainly enjoyed it. ("What have you been doing all your life?" "Thinking.") Intelligence travels light and requires very little energy; in fact it may be sharpened by hunger. (Compare being dulled by corpulence.) And my aching shoulder is trying to tell me that thinking may be the best way to travel.

For the body is what this is all about, as it has been the one imperfect ingredient in my travels. Which it simply cannot be, for wise nomadism is what this is about. Re-inventing the heel. Or maybe the arch support. Must we always be rediscovering principles in order to appreciate them?

May 14: Five ibises just flew into South Dakota. I've never seen even one. This is one of the essential rewards of birdwatching: sitting by the road minding my own news when out of the great blue fly five large dark birds I haven't seen in thirty years on the planet. I should continue south and see what others might be edging this way, to meet them halfway or pass among them. Barn owls, cardinals, Mississippi kites. Boat-tailed grackles. Inca doves.

Into Valentine for an ornithologists' meeting. At the public library I went straight to a dictionary. I'd been wanting to look up nihilism, to see how far I've come from it. *The absurd life is a short one.* Then I looked into guides to edible wild plants. One discusses yucca, and its flower buds I'd been enjoying all week, a few every day with the promise to scatter seeds next time. Their flavor I learn is due to *saponin.* As in soapy, soapweed; a diarrheic. I'm advised not to eat too much. And then it occurs to me. —The wise nomad can ill afford, the food shooting through me as if I'm not even there.

○

Fireflies on the hill above me—summer! you have returned.

"I don't get into the Hills enough."
"That's everybody's problem."

June 2: The first "bad sign" appeared around mid-day, when I found a spruce with its top cut off, and a couple more upstream. It means a road nearby—such slobs wouldn't walk far—and thus an end already to this pristine section of the creek I'd been the morning in walking.

The spruce I assume had been cut for Christmas trees, from last Christmas. Spruce are a favorite for using as Christmas trees, and these dead ones serve well as embodiment and symbol of the Christian ritual: living things sacrificed to celebrate a human god, brought inside as substitute for the real thing, outside. Then they're thrown into some ditch or alley when it's over, the final act of a consumer ritual dedicated more to buying than to giving. This is the Christianity that would replace, and even desecrate, the Indians' pantheism here in its holiest place.

To enter the Hills, then, is to enter with body and mind a living controversy. It is a controversy over one hundred years old, inherited and not to be returned. It crashes ahead, resolved if at all in a sense of finality, in places that also cannot be returned, for being obliterated. It's difficult. And a flatlander like me is tempted to turn around, roll back down with a stream away from these hills and promise not to return, rather than face it.

O

So, plenty of gravity here. One is almost always resisting falling; it was almost never like this on the plains.

I return to the Hills with strings attached to me, from the organs and engines of the culture that nourishes me. I'm thinking through the attachments and trying to dissolve them. I know them well. By driving here I reinforced a host of them, and my reward is to suddenly be here without appreciating the difference. Not like the original visitor, winding my way in along a stream and welcoming these wooded slopes as relief from the plains.

Instead, I looked out at one point this morning and wondered: how do I get over there, a half-mile across a valley, and why? A mile on foot, steep up and down, through thickets of pine, over logs and rock rubble— Already I've thought how puny I must look from above, and feel, from inside, crawling among the trees. Still, it is good after so much grass to be among trees, and myself to scale a shrew among the stems.

The trees are spilling outward from these hills where protected from fire by people. Otherwise they are in a long retreat, twelve thousand years or longer of this place on earth turning into sunnier skies since the last ice age. Then drought and fire became more common than trees as the great forests of the plains were seared and reduced to this cloudcroft island. Now there's only a spider-silk filament of trees remaining along the rivers on the plains to suggest a connection to that wooded past.

In this sense these hills are less forest than refuge for trees. And it is hard to decide if the trees and all the life creep up the slopes, resisting gravity and the extremes near the top, or pour down with the sunlight and rain. Up it must be, against the fall of rock and snow and lightning. But do the tree roots grip or split the rock? Either way the result is the same: more tumbled rocks. Better for trees than for grass? Even then the forest is an opportunity for drought or wind or beetle or lightning—and all at once—all at once—to make these become mere grassy hills on the plains. But the rockiest. And oldest: original rock that's stood long above the mud oozing around them. We're all now sliding off the Rockies.

The hills rise right through the rivers. The more they rise the more they river.

It is such a delirious interplay of elements and forces: continents wind clouds mud seeds ash—without end. Now people are just another.

<u>June 6:</u> As the doing prevails over the telling. Each one suffers for the other until eventually one must give: now perched on the rocks above Pine Creek, waiting for the hawks I'd heard calling this morning to appear in the treetops below, I stop to recount my goods:

There was a common loon at Sheridan Lake, near the spillway. Better yet, I'd anticipated it the day before, imagining the trudge around the lake and hoping for something exotic to rescue it. And since it looks like Minnesota. . . . So now it sounds like it. Prediction is everything.

Then up the dry hillside, cursing the trailmaker who makes us climb Mt. Warner. For a view, I suppose. I like a view but I like water more; couldn't we head up a valley? But I found a gallon jug set by the trail, with a little water in it I need and can filter and trust.

I found two big anthills, three feet high and across. A little patch of sunlight was striking one, and the ants followed it in a cluster through the morning. Sapsucker sign, then a sapsucker, a pair, a nest cavity. One tall ponderosa had a streak of lightning down its trunk, and the sapsuckers had stitched the length of it with holes along either side.

Around Samelius Peak. More splendid trail all to myself. Twice, hen turkeys charged me, defending their chicks I could barely see in the tall grass. Crowded quarters: in a dead elm, a chickadee and downy woodpecker had nest holes just four feet apart on the same limb. I sat in the shade to watch the parents bring food.

Then last night I found this enchanted spot, said look no farther and settled in. A cañon wren called from the rocks above me. This morning I was rewarded with the hawks calling, and a nuthatch quietly feeding its young.

And I have drunk mightily from the streams, filtered and not. Still winter cold.

But my notes from these days do not all cry out for retelling. Rutted trails and robbed streams—the trail robs the stream and the stream washes out the trail. Whether to widen, deepen, or fix the trail? Or cross it at odd angles? At the other extreme a trail passing through a meadow, so faint with disuse it showed only by the grass growing a little shorter there. An ankle twisted by a powerline clearing, bringing me back from the far horizon with force and pain to local ground. Stumps and proposed stumps, bulldozers and slash piles, three men throwing a double axe at an aspen. As the trail turned into a logging road. The aspen in splinters for growing too close.

The birds still singing here. I tell myself this is agriculture, and try to equate a square mile here to one back home. And a better example of farming it is, with a brief harvest disturbance followed by effortless regeneration in relative abandonment, as farming goes. But there is that road, that inroad. And in the Hills that apparently means spurs and shortcuts and connectors. My first impression of the Hills, repeated with each return, is that the roads go everywhere here, up every little valley and along every ridge. Tracks and ruts in telltale parallel, they mock the achievement and spoil the experience in walking there. But a friend of mine, born here, has said, "There are places we couldn't have got to if we hadn't driven there." My point exactly.

The hills are touched all over. Witness this map, of roads and trails only, and not all of them. The print of a heavy and graceless hand, reaching in everywhere, disfiguring. Those who would only drive to

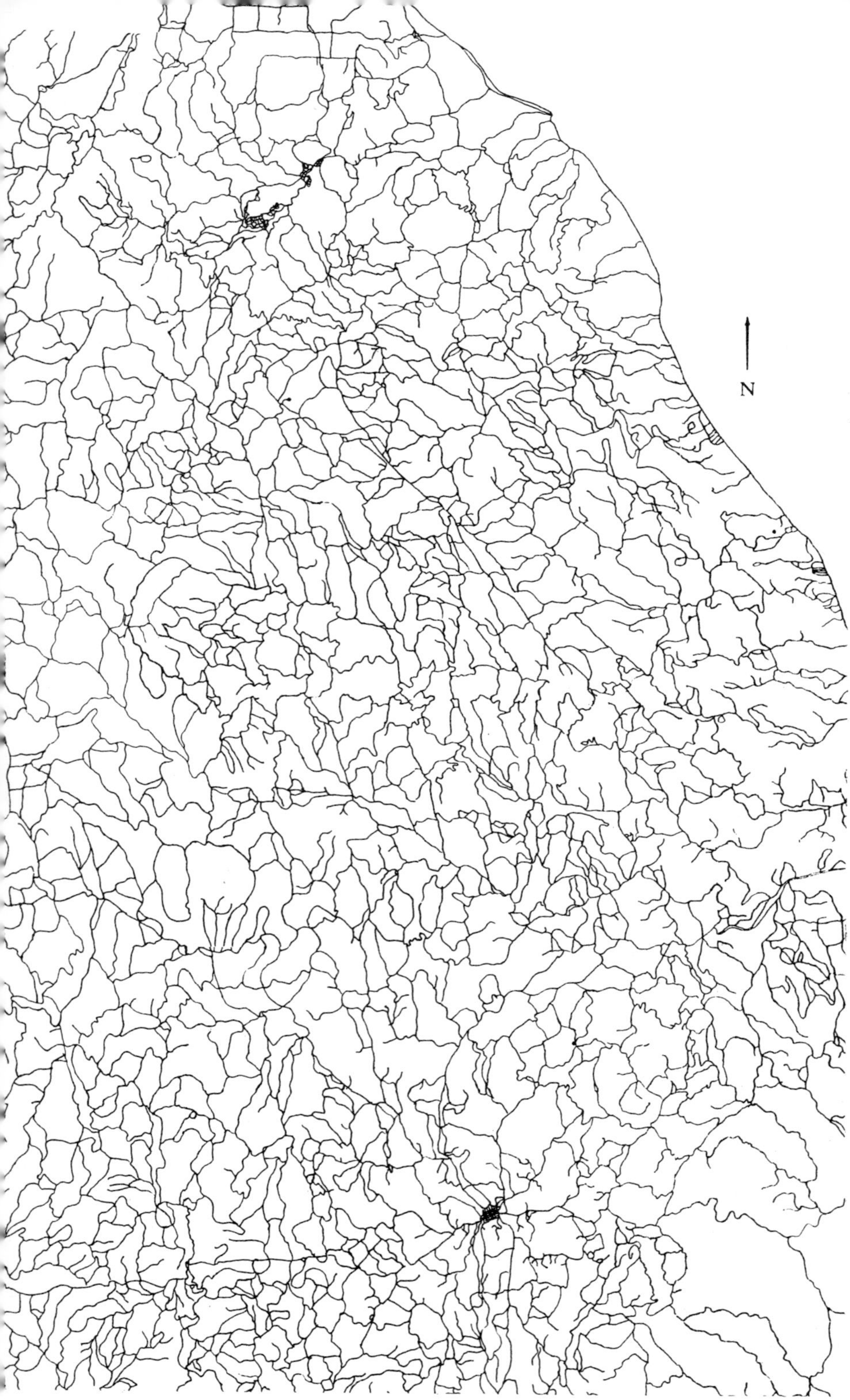
N

be here, the world that in waves runs away. . . rough handling equaled only by my being alone. Again, where is everybody? Just the breeze of a car comes to me from the road a mile away. The road at times is the busiest in the Hills. Half a million people there, one here; one valley hardly communicating with the next; a fine, precarious balance.

June 7: In the Norbeck. A gentle rain this morning: showing my head in an aspen grove, hushed by the sound of rain on leaves. The delight in hearing voices, only voices, of people coming down the trail.

Suddenly alive   among rocks   I am light   feet and hands   all at once straddling cliff and tree   meeting the top of a tree with ease   light as air and a rock wren ringing   water the rock catches tastes of lichen

Tastes of goat, more like. I'd been careful, checking the little catch-basins for turds of any kind, but one I forgot, until I saw little white worms swirling in the wake of my slurp. The dread, deep in the gut: do we share parasites? I wouldn't know. Worry and wishes will make no difference, and later prancing again over the rocks I thought: truly now I am part goat.

○

Beaver dams, trees and trails flooded, a mallard hen with eight chicks. At night, an owl calling over the clearing, echoing off the rocks.

June 8: Yesterday I watched a trout in its favorite pool, always returning to the same position just off a point of the bank, something in the current that held it there. Waiting, wondering: who will yawn first? Today I'll be getting hungry, instead of leaving, and because I kept the trout there in front of me, without reaching for it.

June 10: Was it that wet snow five winters ago that laid these trees down for me to feel crawling and small among the crossed logs, bringing me thirsty to the spring where the deer left its antler, where the dead come to life, with teeth: the squirrel, that porcupine up the hillside: the antler half eaten. I had to come to this place. And others to come, forgotten springs and antlers.

○

Down to the creek and up the other side, away from water and searching for more. I don't have the words for this place as I do for the plains. I'm trying to learn the language of these hills, their grammar of water so it might roll easily onto my tongue.

Another language, sign language, has greeted me almost every place I've been: of trees, especially spruce, red with their bark stripped off. The work of three-toed woodpeckers. But where are they? So much sign, without the signaller. Then this evening I found two woodpeckers where their soft tapping sounds like water, dripping.

And then the sound of real water—

○

But tonight is the lowest full moon in eighteen years, and I'm in one of the deepest canyons in the state. To see the moon I must scale the north side a ways up from here. Do you remember all those years ago, the night like this when the moon rose *there*, and in transit was obscured just *so*, from here? The memory you would need, of place and change and cycle, to follow the moon's orbit. The patience you would have, waiting for this point in the orbit to return.

June 11: Now morning waiting for the woodpeckers to do their own thing, whatever that thing might be. Waiting for it to be revealed. They're here somewhere. Last night it was a duet, their courtship: chasing around, staccato drumming and head dancing. That was at sunset. Not at noon, not this morning yet. A pattern there?

My ignorance knows no bounds. It is a series of blank pages, dated to distinguish them but little more. Today it is three hours since sunrise, and I've heard and seen nothing of the woodpeckers. Nothing that is never nothing but priceless information, here suggesting the woodpecker's true self, its quiet method of dismantling an aging tree.

○

The depths of my anger always awaken me to compassion, but first there is the anger. The way a tangled mess of barbed wire fouls a meadow: my anger and adrenalin overcoming the biting flies to tug cursing at the wire, half-buried, its loops set to rip the tendons of innocent prancers-by, rolling it up and stuffing it beneath a tree, the best that I could do.

June 12: Can't seem to get going this morning. Ennui in the spruce woods, lethargy at 6,000′, one leg always higher than the other—a momentary lapse in stimulation, here, all alone among wooded hills. Monotony resonating from my brain. I suppose throwing myself against a tree is an answer. But it's not necessary to jump into the tree; no, let the tree fall on me. Or the reason not to throw myself at the world is not to do that to the world.

But the day is rescued by a spring, the very river pouring into light and life from the dark of the mountain, by prairiesmoke and giant thistles—fresh greens—by black tea from India. Now the sky begins its mid-day cloud show, with thunderclaps of applause to draw my attention there, to some moment of climax I might otherwise miss. Dancing meadows in the rain.

(That's too bad, to be really doing that.)

Lightning roulette, call it. Maybe rain will mean not dancing but hiding, spruce roulette with astronomical odds. My spruce won't be the spruce that is struck.

The deer will think, this is what people do, or did, dance in meadows.

dancing would mean more of us   only encouraging song sparrows giving true hawk berth

One day field of dandelions, one day wind—today. The plumed seeds floating away, the storm in abeyance, three-toed's courting across the valley.

I hope these flies are everywhere and I only sit among *these* flies. Else they might be an entourage—

June 13: Too bad, again, to be sitting in a meadow full of phlox and phlox cloud: fragrant. The consistency with which I have done well, "had a good time" on my journeys amazes me. It can't be this good, or easy, and all to myself, always. The contradiction of it being so good, yet being alone—

And it could be *easier*, with practice, with a culture to support one. Wouldn't these goods get better, with so many to share? And better for being easier, the burden shared?

It makes me feel good, to be alive. But wouldn't a good universe everywhere perceive itself to be good, and not just through me?

○

Phlox cloud: then butterflies, bees, sedges, *senecio, geum, poa*—I lapse into Latin. It will be like this *verbena* everywhere I go *anemone* still or shuddering meadow *delphinium* original colors *calypso* bluebird sky *virga* hours of trudge *cirsium* leading to moments of joy *vertigo.*

What the Hills are I might be able to say. Sacred to some, home to others, refuge and relict and rare. Silken trees, cold moonlight, the waters flecked with gold. Places you'd go out of your way to leave alone. Berries without the bear. This singular place, hard rock remaining out of the soft plains blowing and flowing around it.

But proposing what the Hills are *for* won't be as easy. A spirit I can't define—breath?—or can't discern, my vision is too poor. Yet it is important to say what they are, and are for, now, before certain answers are closed off from us, and others forced on us.

Gold mining would do that—answer the questions, sweep other answers away, and force others, lesser ones, on us. It is an obligation from the past hanging over us, a promise that may have once made sense but now distorts us: that the minerals will come first. The mineral portion is what these hills are for; their history and form and the life upon them are as nothing to the value of the minerals beneath the surface, the gold and precious metals. Especially the gold. It is as if it had been stored here all these centuries, for us. All else will be swept aside to serve this plunder. We are the ones who allowed this. The technology met the price met the demand: for gold, calamity's metal, today sold mostly as a luxury consumer item, not for food or shelter or other necessities but for coins and jewelry. We're desecrating the earth to ornament ourselves.

It was we who did this. Nothing stopped us.

This is the feeling of discontinuity, of before and after. The forever time behind us now always disconnected from us, the time forever in front of us we hereby agree to. The time before of these rocks rising and falling at their own pace through seas and rivers and fires. The time ahead, of them profoundly and permanently changed. These old, old hills ground to gravel and dumped in their valleys. In a lifetime.

The mining finishes the life and the history of these places. And can we live with ourselves, for so many finished places? So we're severed from our past, and it's much easier on our conscience to bury this place before we learn it too well, and know the difference, and have to decide.

It seems we never hold back, never say, "this place is sacred"—not just 'wildlife refuge' or 'wilderness.' We are tortured to think of the possibility of leaving a place alone for no reasons of our own, not for its beauty or our refreshment but for whatever reasons it may have. No one is saying to the people of the Great Plains, "where are your sacred places?" Where do you say, "we have enough," and start giving back, with gratitude? And for once and this place leave the gold in the ground.

Look at us: we won't give the Hills back to Indians to consecrate but we will give them to miners to desecrate. Our selective allegiance binds us to documents signed in 1872 but not in 1868. This relationship of mining law and treaties is perfect and opposite, our greed and perversion of purpose set against potential generosity and reconciliation. The one forces or allows us to proceed with our pillage without facing the question again—do minerals have priority?—while pushing the affirmative answer. The other asks us to do the honorable deed, and we respond by belatedly declaring war, won fair, and over. To the victors, the spoils. Then we offer cash as settlement, as if it was *material* we are fighting over.

This is a situation we alive now have inherited. It has taken a long while—generations—to arrive here; it may take as long to get out.

Credit or blame does not reach far from my great-grandparents. I am responsible only for my standing here. The Black Hills were never ours to give back, but that we must do: not to any tribe or human entity, but to themselves; not a mere exchange of title, but *dispossession.* Else we'll have learned nothing from our fighting, fighting that tears the hills among us and deserves that no one should own them.

If the pain of this idea is too much, delay it, while accepting it. Let your grandchildren inherit your disinheritance, when you will have passed beyond caring. Or is even that too soon? Then what generation will grow up believing what we can hardly imagine?

June 26: I set off on a bicycle, mountain or is it prairie bike? Wide tires with plastic liners to fend off cacti, the whole to save my feet and shoulders from the life of a draft animal. But I am still able to go cross-country, as slow as I care, even pushing the bike if I wish. The big difference is on hills: uphill I have gears; downhill, planet joy.

○

Prediction is nothing. In April I'd noted, "it's a clover year," referring to all the little clover plants at my feet. But I didn't know what I was talking about, not this endless thicket, thick and tall, thick, tall, thick, thick. In pastures it's everywhere, usually not so dense that I can't pedal through it but in places, especially low places—by the Cheyenne—it grows so rank and tall I can barely get through it or see over it. I look for the oft-cursed cow paths, well-grazed areas, dry spots—walking would have been no easier.

This year every place is remote. I'd like to go over to those cottonwoods over there, but why bother? If I am to record faithfully my place and time then June will have to be written in clover. Fragrant and yellow in bloom, it is an imposition on the land, really, for being non-native, introduced from Europe. It is biennial, so the seeds of this conflagration must have sprouted last summer or fall. I don't know if it is so strictly so, if we can expect the odd-numbered years henceforth to be so graced or beset by clover—but think of us, wherever you are, in those odd years—

It makes for a simple world, the yellow earth embracing a blue and white sky. But there was a moment today—I'd just crossed a fence and looked up from the valley at the yellow bowl of hills around me—it's hard not to be cheered by so much yellow, and with a fresh breeze bringing the cloud shadows towards me down the hillside—all at once I was sure my telling would be unequal to the tale. You will be unimpressed or unbelieving, and it will be all my fault.

June 27: One does not live here long without looking for a southeast-tending in the land and the things on the land, driven by the dominant north to northwest wind. Here being the northern plains, but especially around the Hills. How old is this wind? How long has it been blowing around those rocks, hastening down the east side and forcing the creeks, which would flow east, south? These old creeks pinwheeling round the Hills.

Or find the northwest wind written in the smallest things of the land, like windshaped patterns in the ground's leafy cover. Everything would like to radiate. Wind pushes it into a fan, or advances it in waves, corduroy fashion, the ground itself so moved. The grass in waves advancing reveals the wind, as the wind in waves highlights and names the grasses.

Wind is given, rigid, unpredictable, extreme. Small wonder it should shape and organize whole continents and least coulees.

straight trees whirlwinds
straight winds whorled trees

○

This afternoon I thrashed my way up to a spring, hoping to find less laxative water. I followed the streamcourse mostly, where the clover hadn't taken root. This gave me a choice between clover and mud. At the spring I found deep mud, deceptively dry-capped. With black shale mud over one ankle I took a different route down, a round trip: mud above the other ankle. Mud and the rank and tangled clover growing there, stumbling crashing down I went, the heat the dusty clover on and on choking grunting breathing more out than in. Is this how the land feels?

June 28: This morning I took to a gravel road.

Mid-day heading north over the flats west of the Cheyenne I was awakened by a pipit singing. I mean, awake and riding then aroused from that state by a sound, a distinctive, *tinkling*, heard-before *bells*. Really awake now I ditched my bike with a motion and walked into the pasture and gave myself over to it.

Lying back to squint at the bright clouds to find it, I do, a tiny dot of a bird circling way up there. Yet its voice seems to surround me. It is a legendary ventriloquist, but that hardly explains this far, small thing singing in my ear.

Half a mile on, another one.

When I come upon any animal I've learned to freeze, slowly crumple to the ground and try to disappear, then look for a way around it. It is one kind of learning, perhaps arbitrary; has become habit. Until now I want not to disturb but to be passing merely. Don't show my face or eyes, and certainly not my teeth. "People walk by," the animals will think.

My next thought is wanting more. If two pipits why not four? We do not live in a rain forest and so welcome these beings as few as they are far between. We want more. Could we ever get enough? Too much? Imagine becoming inured to an intense, vibrant landscape.

There is the possibility that the spaces between pipits might grow larger—

June 29: I set myself out as an open page for the earth to write with, whatever it might propose, incident there. And hoped it wouldn't be snakebite, encephalitis, rabies.

○

Out of the valley and onto the flat. Again. My washboard ride. Here the pastures give way abruptly to fields, and the immediate, perverse feeling of realizing something's presence as soon as it's gone. The birdsong ends. Days full of it had prepared me for this, to arouse me. A person blind, or blindfolded, could map this land with birdsong. As valleys, breaks, and flats, since there is a pattern here of growing alfalfa in the valleys, grazing the breaks, and farming the flat tables. And each would announce itself with sound: the long summer days of birdsong in the pastures versus silence, and the occasional noise of farm implements, in the fields.

"Rain follows the plow" went the hoax, and now it appears the plow follows the road. The many times in my life I've seen the pavement begin and the pastures end—along with the birds. Actually, it's more a lockstep of grain trucks and pavement increasing, growing to fill the available level ground, like lungs or rivers shaped, branching to cover a table. Topography, it appears, is destiny.—As the Great Plains now display this pattern throughout. Or soil is destiny, and very little pays to pave the hillsides.

I'm not sure if I can point to a good reason, except this difference in birdsong, why I've come to prefer the pasture to the field. Something about the rich variety within the prairie, versus the monotony of farmland. And that it's not uncommon to celebrate the rare, as when farmland becomes the rule and the prairie a remnant. I suspect I wouldn't want to live there, in the one without the birds.

So I would like to step outside, not defend or criticize this development but merely report it. Out of all the possibilities, I've come to be sensitized to farmland. I overlook a region and evaluate it in those terms, distinguishing the farmers' stripes and false green squares from the ranchers' speckled calico. And once the wild, shifting calico begins I wish it would never end, such places as my eyes can graze on easily, and eagerly, horizon-round. Neck-craning country. At the other places, with field after farmless field, I cringe in turning my head in apprehension of what I'll see. But it is not surprising, given my time and place, that someone would grow up and realize where he is living. It's as if the prairie had reawakened through me—

June 30: You may think I *gush*, exaggerate even, but too often I catch myself trying to understate what a thrill natural form and color are.

If I could just stare. Some of the best times I've had were just staring. Seeing *through* vision. Looking *at* the eyes instead of with them, scanning the sight with the brain.

Alas, to see you must blink.

To become accustomed to anything is sad. The way birdsong inevitably becomes background, or the brain the servant of the eyes. And I cannot decide if one would be better, to accustom to the best or worst of times or places. In either case missing it, so used to the sight we look right through it. Not only "out here" where the beauty is unconcealed, but in our everyday lives missing what is there. Accustoming as resignation, adaptation, habit: the lowering of eyelids and expectations. Accustoming to the worst in ourselves. Missing it.

July 1: A back to earth's a back not turned: as it is in lying face-up at the base of a cottonwood, the tree apparently rooted in the brain. The new view so the old stories can't start up, and new ones can begin.

All the universe fits inside my brain; earth hides half of it. Not to hold it against the earth. No, I'm more inclined to hugging it. This would be the ultimate connection, lying back, not in sloth but in economy. Rich in ideas. The feeling of being absorbed, becoming big, the body stretching out mentally through the skin to embrace the earth, and think for it. In case it needs assistance.

hug the earth hug yourself hug the earth hug yourself

July 2: Down by the river the clover is turning to grasshoppers—other yellows. They've stripped the clover of leaves and flowers to the lank stem, and mornings and evenings they climb to the top—sun worshippers—and appear to displace the flowers, like an odd, lumpish-flowered thicket. Birds appear—more yellows—and pick the flowers. Is it good fortune or mere effect, that the meadowlarks are so well organized along the river this time of year?

Down by the river two separate voles had wandered onto the mud of a yazoo stream, become mired, and died there. *The flies that bind.*

July 3: Riding over the flat south of the Cheyenne I was approached by six long-billed curlews. *Accosted* might be a better word, *strafed*, even, to describe their diving screaming flights at my head. It isn't fair; if I'd been passing by this family in a car at any speed they would have barely noticed me.

If I'd been by in a car I might not have noticed them. And at my cycling pace I cannot miss the dead birds, what the road kills, along the road. I always stop for them. I do not count them but only look into their eyes and wonder at their one life before lofting them into the ditch. —Their last flight that isn't, heavily back to earth, the wound closing on itself.

It's that time of year, with all the young birds, nesting successes, crisscrossing the roads. Their luck is blind, their nemesis not. They are not only symptom and symbol but direct result of our hurtling through the world, a passing-through that is there the least but takes the most, leaving the maximum trail, not noticing much less recognizing the birds by species or season.

Oh, this would be another way to map the world, with great iron hulks hurtling along and sucking in a certain volume. If the flow of autos was constant we could gauge something about the animals' numbers, by place or time: kingbirds by the shelterbelts, swallows round the bridges, frogs and coons in the low places, grouse and pheasants by cornfields in winter. We could also learn something about the animals' population cycles. The more we find dead, the more must be alive—up to a point. If instead the animals were what we knew we might guess something about the traffic, the price of its fuel, the state of its economy. . . .

count the birdsong between your steps
count less

I rendezvoused with a friend at Philip and we drove into the night, into the east, camped and waking in the Orient Hills: the rising sun seems to have grown larger during the night.

July: *Another kind of winter: hot. And it's time we got these glaciers out of the way. In one sweeping image they will stand for all that is cold and flat about the plains. And maybe this place is always only more or less under the ice, only in-between ice epochs, and any winter might be the snowball's start to an interminable icy regime. If so the land is ready for it.*

⊙

Are we the earth's first people to realize a sense of our place among the stars? First to recognize our luck in coming of age in this interglacial period, first to anticipate its ending? Our colonization of this brief sunny morning.

It's incredible if we're on a schedule, with a renewed glacial period anytime in the next 10,000 years. Maybe soon. So it's hard not to look for signs, impending, and hard not to find them. Some winters do pass for glacial, starting in October or November with an ice and snow storm that seals the earth from the warmth of the sun. *Snowbound, with the snow driven south on the wind.* This mirrored coat preserves itself and increases, forcing its way through March and April—blizzard season, when we can have no doubt of the snow's ability to accumulate, predominate, and endure.

The ice is visible also in the still landforms, impressed or embossed and now even rebounding from the ice. Continental glaciers like the ones that visited here are far off any comprehensible scale. It's one thing to look over this valley full of air, quite another to imagine ice there. It's hard to conjure up a thousand feet of ice in place here in front of me. It may have been ten thousand feet thick, in places; maybe far north of here. Here at the edge of the ice these hills were merely the ice's muddy boots.

So much land so moved, by water in its frozen state. We here now don't have nearly enough winter for such an undertaking. The glaciers weren't our doing. They came out of the north and brought winter with them. It's the planet's thing, after all, in the turning of the earth and sun. It's not our fault that it's flat and cold here; it may even be a source of credit.

The flatness means we are most nearly concentric, most perfectly round. What other surfaces on earth are shaped just so?

Oceans.

No one of us stands much higher, or much closer to the center.

Here the rain can actually flow down, towards the center of the earth, at least a while before it slips off some tilted layer underground.

. . . and whatever the land lacks by its flatness is made up for with sky. . . .

In practice, in the valley, the levelness means you often have to go right up to a stream to ask which way it's flowing. Even then it might not make sense, as some tributaries aim north before emptying into the James flowing towards them. The low hills along the valley are themselves a jumble, where the ice left an unsorted mass of rocks and dirt behind. I've done that, too. My boots now hold more clay and more life than the icecap ever had. Grass hills. Gentle. Level on another scale, there's so much up-and-down but no obvious *down.* In practice, they puddle. Ponds and potholes large and small, rock-rimmed and salt-stained, pans set out to catch the rain.

○

still glacial, without much cause to run off the water moves in sheets, rilles, the barest minimum words for flow. oozing, pressured. slight. still.

○

Some peoples may have known this valley as a lobe of ice, a cold blinding peninsula with muddy summers around it. More recently there was a great shallow lake in the ice's place, and a river slipping from it. In time the lake filled and dried, leaving a river the length of its valley to name. So the James River is too young—less than a thousand generations—to have had many names. Not enough cultures have swept over it, claiming and naming. —Naming the sediments, for they are what this valley is: rocks of all sizes, boulders and silt, plucked and carried along by the ice, rolled and rounded and abandoned. There hasn't been time for polishing.

Sediment becomes soil under the tutelage of grass and trees; ten thousand years they've had to make this valley fertile for the ones who call it James to settle and farm for fifty years, then farm and unsettle for the next fifty. Which brings us to today.

This farming is another kind of glacier: creeping and slow, tearing up the surface and redistributing the rocks left by the last of the ice. This glacier rode *up* the valley, favoring first the level places and overriding last the rocky hills alongside. It is a kind of desert while in place. It still loses its finest part, the finest soil, to winter winds and spring snowmelt, often in tandem.

This new glacier also scoured the ground, plucking the rocks one by one and arranging them in discrete piles at the edges or centers of fields. Much energy in hands, hooves, and tractors went to recollect what the ice scattered. The rocks haven't seen this much action for a long while and probably won't again soon: we now have the energy to rebury the rocks, but all in one place.

Burial, forgetting and change, and the rocks may be the least of it. Gone also is the prairie, *the* prairie, one of the world's great grasslands dug up, turned over to rot and planted to grains. Farmed more or less annually ever since. What goes through the mind of the farmer who wakes one day and sets out to break new ground, ground he may have known all his life? *The pasture.* When was the decision made, and made hard, so no second thoughts occur even after the tool first strikes the earth? Was any man made sick by the work? Or do those twin killers, ignorance and arrogance, let him rest well at night?

Does the farmer sense the life of the land as he buries it alive? What is it like for the bird or turtle or butterfly as the tractor passes the first time? If it lives it can move on, learn a new angle to the sun and place on the earth—which is already occupied and defended dearly. Outcast and forlorn, that's what it's like. In desperation, blue eggs laid in the dirt.

From the prairie's point of view human pioneering has never ended, and only pauses during winter to refuel. A thousand times a hundred years, individual farmer's decisions have erased a lot of land, or history—same thing— And the grasslands are gone for gluten.

I'd rather not think these things. This passion for prairie would be inhuman if my intention was to make people feel bad about settling, farming, and persevering here, when I mean more to challenge leaving here, by celebrating living here. After all, the prairie's demise has coincided lately with a departure of people from the country: while the prairie in this part of the Plains has been unraveling for 150 years it's really been coming apart recently, which is when the greatest population decline has occurred. Whatever the relationship between the trends—the plowing may have fed the leaving, or followed from it—the two losses, of people and place, must at least be set side by side, as this place becomes unlivable and unlived-in. *A ghost state.* Change in the landscape with few left to live with it. Sometimes it does seem unnaturally quiet out here, especially compared to the stories I've heard older people tell about the wildlife and social life here in the past. There was a time when the two were more in balance, and it was when there were more people. Now we all remember so many people who are gone. Thinking back only on my thirty years here I realize that growing up here has also meant knowing so many places that are gone. Farmsteads razed and plowed under. The pastures around that I knew by heart. Places in the grass a friend and I would hug and explore. There have been too many times I've been asked to leap almost bodily past grief into acceptance, for the places and times in my memory that were erased one morning and now are irrecoverable.

Consider the prairie, figure the wildlife, count the people. Now subtract them all. This would be a mere lament against progress if what had replaced them was an improvement. "Fewer farmers farming more land" is another way to say it. And as these farms become virtual one-man factories the landscape is becoming one only a dirt-farmer could love, with little life but what the farmer allows. Dormant or dead—stubble fields—eight months of the year, it's planted to a monoculture of grains for the growing season. This culture of relentless grain fields supports only what can adapt to its monotony, and to its cyclic disruptions of planting and harvest. The ones adapted are few, if sometimes plentiful: pests. The quantity of life may be the same as ever, but its quality has changed. Monoculture begets monoculture. Diversity takes too much time, too much space. So it seems perverse that a spacious and timeless landscape like the Plains has become less wild and diverse, qualities more to be expected around growing urban areas. An industrial landscape. Unlivable as it becomes unlived-in, and the seasons come and go in silence, with no one to notice or remember.

So the old adage just gets worse: who will want to stay down on such farms? Who will want to do the work? For certainly some of the exodus from the country has been people choosing to leave, not all forced out by economics or bad luck. Leaving the work. It will always include thankless, mindful, back-making tasks, dirty and dangerous and tiring. Mechanization saves labor but adds new dangers, and makes the work noisy, greasy, monotonous—the long hours, the endless rounds, alone. What drives us to do it? What drives us away?

It's easier for some than for others to turn their backs on a place. So this is addressed to the backs of the ones who've left, who cannot remember what they never knew (clear water running through grass), who would rather not know what this farming is doing to the land as it spoils them with easy food. It's hard enough to describe the situation here to ones who know about it. Ones who know, for instance, what it means to nurture a garden carefully. So they can try to imagine how that care necessarily changes and is lost at the scale a farmer works: large machinery and large featureless fields. Larger fields and fewer farmers mean that less attention is given to each acre, and each acre is freer to erode downstream and downwind. Our poor soils are yet Iowa's rich ones. The loss of soil continues despite all we've learned, and all our sad history of dust bowls and eroded gullies. It's as if we haven't learned that droughts happen, wind is a given, and the wind often comes before the rain. Our land only more or less dusty. And the rain, when it comes, is often too much at once for the land to absorb. Now when the waters become undrinkable and the air unbreathable there are few here to complain besides the perpetrators.

More than soil has rolled out the southeast corner of this state. Young people have, also, and the place is the poorer without them as it is for the soil spent to pay their way. Again, subtract the prairie, the people and the soil, ask what they've all been for, and try this answer: *the surplus*. It's the annual rite at harvest time, with grain bins overflowing and grain prices falling. Farming is still a noble calling, producing success like no other as the food piles up, more in one year than any farmer could ever eat. Merely adding more material to a surplus makes farming seem absurd. That the grain would be worth less without government support makes it even more ludicrous. And on the scale that's developing here and around the world the farming has become obscene. It has mutated into an elaborate system of pouring money through soil to produce protein, in excess. Or maybe pouring nitrogen through soil to buy more nitrogen. Money with nothing better to do looks for land to exploit, and large acreages are obliterated at once. This is not done out of love for land, labor, or the food produced. This is agribusiness, emphasis on the business. This is all around the world. And the living part—the land and plants and animals—becomes a mere appendage grafted to a machine for mass production: monstrous.

Justifying this by saying "we feed the world" goes only so far when you're actually feeding the world's livestock. —That is, much of the grain goes to feed animals for slaughter, which may make meat protein available to more people but also condemns more land to the plow, because so much is lost converting vegetable protein to meat—especially when some of those animals could be eating grass, keeping land safe from the plow and thereby doing without much of the elaborate system.

No, we're bringing in the bread for people who live by bread hardly at all, and then eat only half, the soft half, of the kernel. Does easy food make easy people? Or people easy, enjoying a rich banquet without respect for the real labor the food requires and allows? Are we selling our land and labor cheap for undervalued grain? Are we sending the soil downstream and downwind to overproduce to feed lots of animals and pollute the streams that need to be cleaned to wash down the food that's underchewed and overeaten to power the exercise machines?

What all these losses have been for doesn't make up for the losses. This is the part that is hardest to accept.

⊙

Each year is new. All your years' experience can't tell you which of the various winds lies over the horizon. So how can any individual farmer *not* go all-out every year, not knowing whether the seasons will smile or frown on his only acres? Drought years aside, this system of solo farmers maximizing production to minimize their risk produces a regular surplus of grain, annually depressed crop prices, perennial calls for government help, continual crisis in the country— It should be easier for the ever-fewer farmers to cooperate and control their production and hence the price, but even if they could, the buyers—the grain companies—would gladly look elsewhere—overseas—for the grain and the farmers to grow it. It seems we are damned either way, overproducing or controlling production. From here this dismal system spirals out of control around the world, includes ours and the Argentine prairies in one breath and foretells no end in this flowing to the sea.

Place takes time. Without memory to hold it the land slips away. The ones who don't remember may not miss it, but the land misses them. There was a time when it was more alive here for all of us. It could be that way again. The prairie has proven it can support abundant life while creating soil. How can we, too, make the land increase while supporting our lives here? What will make it possible?

August 3: I set out by bicycle again up a familiar frogged valley. (The wet places are still ringing from last year's rain.) Faulk County straddles the slope between the low hills and the river plain, from the great anonymous wheatfields to the west and humid regiments of corn to the east. Not quite in either, it's not lost to either: the creeks that connect in their narrow curving valleys have defied the tractor's rule, and still conduct some elements of the prairie soul into the future, if not downhill.

Today the hawks are competing for air space all along the creek. Herons seem more relaxed—if birds could saunter. . . . In the silence of a herons' rookery I found a lightning-struck ash tree. A fresh white gash in the tree was matched by great chunks of wood on the ground—*in* the ground, as in a powerful display one piece was driven like a lance into the ground.

August 4: Evening, or past: the time when you start looking to the moon for sunlight. Calm evening again, and I want to be everywhere, fly over these hills, the Lebanon Hills only a day's ride away—tomorrow. Unlikely. The day will take it out of me, the sun and wind conspire to discourage me. I'll come upon some sweet neck of a valley and stop. As today I went swimming in a splendid pond near where the harriers nested. (Apparently three eggs hatched and are now flying around.) The swim was all the shade I contrived today, but for a cloud and a hill and my hat. We live for the evenings, the long hot day's reward.

An honest "treeless plain" day. There was one place where I looked south up hill after grassy hill, into monotony, hot and bright. It was plain how the pioneers could lose their senses, all alone, in a dry year, with the wind the only feature of the plain. Approached with the right state of mind, however, even the ground becomes exciting. I was sitting there when some spectacular green iridescent beetle came rambling towards me. I see I have been traveling much too fast, I should have been crawling, and wonder now what I might have missed these past months. How can I claim to be true to the earth, at this rate? True to the ground: varied, patterned, colored, living, moving; stones. A great carpeted room lit by weather.

I was there when a whirlwind crossed still water. The sound, of rubbing, ripping air, drew me to it, as a pattern like a shuddering lipprint on the water.

August 5: The hills are connected, more or less, nearly the length of the state between the glacial plain and Missouri River. I deliberately ride among the hills because they are less farmed, for being hilly, rocky, and poorly drained. The roads occasionally roll me off, but I faithfully ride back up at the first opportunity.

We live in a time when prairie is gone, yet celebrated inversely to how much is gone. Just as when it was all here few appreciated it and many cursed it. They may have known it better than we do; we may have the temperament to restore that intimacy without being overwhelmed by it.

To find a remnant of original, undisturbed prairie is to appreciate immediately the cause for celebration, especially today when the remnants stand out amidst the farmland like pages of verse in a book on economics. The sight of grass at your feet and reaching out of view in all directions is real and rare and irreplaceable, one of this planet's great understated experiences. The charm is that the soul of the prairie can be found even in a small remnant.

Yet in all this attention to grass has anyone noted the look of ripe grass, on blonde hilltops backlit by the evening sun? Where is it *written?* Or the way ripe golden grass makes silver footprints of the person walking before you in the moonlight. (You can circle round and see your own.) And the look of tall grass, waving in all the winds: the gentle winds come like a light traveling over the grass. Like a light, it is light, as the grass stems flex, reflex, and reflect, slipping back into the wind left by the other stems.

Grass is sun-shaped, wind-driven, fire-hardened, and rain divining.

○

Grass in moonlight—anything in moonlight—loses its color and identity and name, so its form is all the eyes can apprehend. Patterns of form and patterns of pattern can freely approach the light-trained and name-loving brain. So a walk by moonlight can be enlightening: these plants, say bluegrass or snowberry, become instead the place where the ground turns to sod, or raises woody stems in patches. There, on the north side of that steep hill, the shadow *is* trees.

August 6: These lone cottonwoods—everyone knows at least one—spaced out along some streamcourses, *tell* where the water is. I drink the water the cottonwood drinks. Water is our one weakness. So obviously made from water, their branches droop towards it, barely able to rise to the sun. Their waxen clapping leaves make a liquid sound, and a pool of shade that fills with lush grass.

On starless full moon nights the shiny leaves catch the moonlight and turn it into stars.

These lone cottonwoods. What brings them here must carry them forward: near each one I look for the log of the last one, grandmother to the young one I look for downstream. One long lonely generation at a time spiraling through the wind towards the sun. And their physical appearance, the proportion, once you know it, of roots to branches: a mass of roots belowground feeds a relative scrub of a plant above, and suggests the soil is stable and nurturing, but meager, while the air is intense and rich, but severe.

○

There's nothing that can force appreciation of what's happening to the land, by farming or other activities, like having to drink the water that flows from it. But if I'm stupid for drinking the waters filtered have the herons any chance at intelligence?

August 7: If it was "coyotes every night" back in May then it's been the smell of death every day here in August. Most often from some cow or calf, reaching the peak of decay and wafting to me on a breeze.

Sometimes it all boils down to one word. I mean, seeing that word conjures it all up: all the fences I've crossed, the abandoned tangles of wire, the trampled springs and woods and shores, the stink in the wake of cattle trucks, the cattle prodded and packed in there, the stench of feedlots, the cattle there, the odor of rotting flesh, burning meat, as the flesh becomes meat—that one word seen on a plastic wrapper stuck in the grass: *smokies.*

August 8: Squawking led me there, to seven dark night herons roving south against the sundown. The air has wings. I look for the upbeat, and count the day's third owl by its call.

We had a fabulous view of the moon tonight, the same ever fabled summer moonrise. The moon's fully opposite the sun now, and appeared over yet another elegant line of grassed hills lit by the orange sky that held the herons. Later the moon took over the sky and the solar system became plain: everything in circles: the sun over my right shoulder, the moon tied to my belly; Saturn and Jupiter there and there, distant. This is how it would look if we could float in space without the earth. *The earth is my body, lucid to me.*

August 9: The world teaches exhaltation. I learn by immersion. It's mighty persuasion.

August 10: The south wind came on with the sun but did not leave with it: tonight I am lying low, in a place where the trees amplify the wind in absorbing it. Deafening but calm, it's real shelter, although it doesn't sound like it: a small pond encircled by willows and cottonwoods. Some other day's rain is dampening today's wind.

Whatever the wind is, it takes it out of me. If the self is a center with no edges then the wind gives it an edge, and sets to fraying it. It keeps my self very local even as it blows bits of me away to distant parts. The senses collapse into the body, which feels wrapped-up, immersed in sensation but somehow deprived of it. The skin feels so much, but nothing intelligible. *Dry.* Attempts to connect with anything more distant than skin are forlorn—with sound? Full of sound empty of meaning. Smell? Each breath is a mixture compiled from samples of air over a million places both near and utterly far. Eyes are the only organ that can make sense out of the wind, by piercing it. Even then the horizon ripples, as if moving, or watery. Illusive. And at night the stars seem remote, faded and blinking from all the air passing between us. This being so close to myself day after night after day—it gets too close, and I seek a little calm in which to expand my margins without being blown away.

August 11: Again the south wind. This is as trying as any ordeal yet on these journeys. Riding uphills in the lee is actually some relief, until I reach the crest all pooped and am welcomed by a blast—then virtually creep downhill. I should have turned north to see if I could have been blown uphill. Instead, after fifteen miles into it I tacked east, against my southwest plans—there are more routes east than west here, as if the latter was the poorer side of the hills.

I shaded the afternoon away by a lake graced by pelicans. The wind off the lake was cooling, and the waves angling into my cusp of shore faded, turned, and came straight on: the wind circling around to come out of the north. I rode on.

August 12: Rainbows are fewer this year than last. Rainbows are pure extravagance, although necessary to a sky that holds air and water and light. But what am I to make of their absence, except another sign that the year's been dry.

So last night was my first real storm of the summer, and I was out in it. I could have hidden by trees or corn or haystacks but instead I found an open grassy spot to set my tent. The dark clouds amassing in the west showed no gap at the horizion to allow the sunset and signal the storm's ultimate impotency. Then the vigil, waiting in the dark for my turn at the storm's mercy. And surely it came, wind and rain and lightning. And surely I survived, holding the tent down with my body and trying to keep my eyes open to the lightning. If I was to be struck at least I would see it. It was hard—some struck within a quarter mile—very hard to keep them open.

Thunderstorms are the earth in one of its most intensely chaotic moments, most able to sweep me under the surface: not at all "designed for me if I could but see," but impersonally testing me just to stay alive.

Then today in an abandoned farmhouse I found an old, pigeon-stained copy of Muir's *Stickeen.* It was left on a shelf just inside the door, as if to be found. I went outside and sat in the grass to read it, a gripping tale of Muir and the little dog Stickeen on an Alaskan glacier in a rainstorm. The glacier a "prairie of ice;" the storm, "God making landscapes." When Muir described looking into the dog's eyes, "as old as the hills, and as young, and as wild" I thought, "It's Thoreau! Reincarnate."

○

august by a long lake

a fox lay in a gap of the plum ring
a fox lay in the grass and left plum seeds

August 13: Evening by another lake, where I'm waiting to see the last swallow leave the air over the water. For the second time this year a group of deer came up behind me where I sat. They stomped, hard, wheezed emphatic *hmmh's*, and stomped some more. Their close approach suggests they don't see seated forms often enough to recognize and ignore. This time when I felt their stomping I recognized it and knew enough not to move, not to turn and see them until they were striding away. They didn't learn about fear from me.

○

He said it, not me, and I couldn't have said it better: In a cafe in White Lake I could hear two farmers talking from across the room. One was telling of a recent visit to his in-laws who live by Sisseton. He lamented the way the farming is done there, saying, "That country's all broke up. It's kinda sorry. Kinda sorry."

○

Henry David, Stickeen, we've come so far from the world you knew and loved and traveled through. Would you recognize any of it, today? And leave, heartbroken? Yet many places still have charm. Our world is tamer but no less wild. Thirst still edges out hunger. Wonders do not cease. The golden light at the end of the day still is.

August 14: Would it be too much to say of these nights that I close my eyes on the stars and open them to the sun? Or enough to say so many nights the last I looked on was stars. The spectacle on earth leads me to them, looking for explanation. Because this planet is the sun's thing, which is the galaxy's, which is. . . .You get the picture. Or do you? Each night we turn away from the sun long and well enough to get a good look at the stars, but who looks, anymore? When a glance will do, especially in that time of year when night and winter are indistinguishable. But even these brief, bright summer nights allow us the sensation of being exposed to space, and to imagine what it would be like to be floating without the earth. Then we may appreciate the sun and earth and their perfect relationship, with night, cold night everywhere but towards the sun. If it were a distant star—

I come to the earth through the stars. There may be no truer way. Looking back from the cold dark dust between the stars to life here on earth, that so much and this so little: the farther we go out on that scale the more precious this earth becomes.

"A wonderful sameness" is how Theodore Roosevelt described the plains. Surely he meant full of wonder more than merely good? Now our universe stretches out before us in spectacular uniformity and mass. Spectacle is all it is, more astonishing than good, for as much as is within our reach, or reaches us.

But it does provide a sound and sobering point of view, from "above". Forget it and the earth may become overlarge, so large as to seem limitless, and little marred by our diggings. Or is it really the pettiness of our acts to the scale of the universe that makes us want to enlarge or inflate them, blustering about in trying to refute or undo that imbalance? But this will always be one mighty and overruling planet. Our works can never outstrip the earth. They can never become large. We don't have to try.

You owe us a river.
A river's a lot to owe.

<u>*September 14:*</u> Fog nets, the trees drip. I'd forgotten about this kind of rain, this method of straining the night's air for its dew. All the living things come forth to drink in the clouds.

To one always looking for patterns among even the earth's least things the fog presents a challenge: patterns in the mist? From within, the fog is like a shroud, and familiar sensual certainty vanishes into thick air, replaced by silence, mood, magic: what I can't see can't be commonplace.

I'm always amazed this can be found so near the city. —The magic, that is. Yet this should cause no surprise: it begins at the edge, the bright sunset edge of the city that everyone has seen and turned away from.

○

driving through the evening,
the calm and quiet evening,
    remember how you roar

○

<u>*September 15:*</u> Another morning washed clean. Waking into this fog always feels like absolution, as if my innocence was restored. Or at least it gives me pause and patience. The horizon is brought close, and there's no hurry to reach the edge of my awareness. Exploration in this realm means not the laborious bringing close of far things but the sudden appearance of near things unimagined a moment before.

These calm mornings with the fog wrapped tight around everything I imagine the clouds around the swallows warmed by their bodies, wherever they roost. And discrete pockets of air I could encircle with my arms.

Last night the air was so empty of sound a single meadowlark did fill it. They sing again, in reprise of an overture, and the summer's a movement, movement in-between.

Two springs we have, if the fall is wet. Fall is a confusing season, what with interjections of spring (birdsong and fog), as if it was never too late to start again. (Instead it just gets too cold.) Yet this season like spring is as much cool as it is wet—cool enough to let moisture linger in the ground and the air. Two springs: one warm and melting, sunlit flames licking north over five months of ice while the other has cold air rolling south by night over the warm humid earth. The result is the same: fog.

September 16: Clear this morning. Enough gray sunrises and blue sky will be a relief.

Grouse clucking around me. Grouse wings pound the air *so hard*—evading the harrier. Wave after wave appears, if I look. The wing's slight mixing of the air. What is new is that here we go again.

A fat time for spiders: there's architecture everywhere in the ripe grass, no wind, and the cold flying things.

It is always more or less fall, more or less spring. One can find fall colors in any season, although in summer they are washed out by greens. Some part of some plant is always fading. The prairie—true prairie—has the colors, too. In contrast to being among trees, the closer you get here the stronger the colors become. Around every marsh now concentric rings of color show where each plant or plant community grows, each with a specific need for water, and a characteristic color exposed as the water recedes. Green leaves, revealing the colored bands. The fall comes early from drying.

Like stopping for tea and pissing to put out the fire, or moving a gopher mound to smother it, I want the world to work through me as I walk through it. I conform to its shape, the shape of sustenance.

O

A final book as no other can competes with all the others.

September 17: This much is easy: I've hitchhiked forty miles east of and nearly five hundred feet above the James River. Hills and glacial lakes again, more of the ice cap's unmistakable, inscrutable presence: I still can't envision it. The glacier left the land as a map in three (or more) dimensions, then left no legend as a key. Yet if ever there was an intelligible shape to the land, one to make the ice imaginable, it is this pointed heap of hills, an arrow aimed north against the coming winter. Few places translate from land to map to mind as well as this V wedged into the ice sheet's southern edge. It's as if the ice lost its convection here in a southern clime, and was easily divided. The hills' head is fifty miles north of here, north against the season. With perhaps more conviction than sense I head for that point.

September 18: Real life, slipping through the hills. My driver yesterday reminded me that pronghorns have been re-introduced to these hills. My *antelope clothes* I thought, glad to have them with me, dressed for the occasion.

On some maps these hills show more lake than land. From the ground it seems there's a pond or slough everywhere I turn, one for every hillcrest. Imagine what it's like for birds of water flying south now, to find the earth rising five hundred feet towards them with an offering of moon-silvered ponds. At nights I'll listen to the flocks, to hear if I can detect some tone of recognition or even praise in their voices.

where you find oak trees

it's hard to forget the object of your search,
chasing the jay for its blue.
eludes you as you draw near.

September 19: I've taken shelter in an abandoned country school—shelter from rain. I made a fire on scrap tin—you would have me burn a hole in the floor?—and brewed some tea and am drying out and warming up. Me and a fire in this country school—surely the variety of human experience is endless? Surely joy is relative? Or what was that I felt, coming out of a cold driving rain into mere clouds and wind, and what could have compounded that joy? A ray of sun, I suppose. And so forth, to the upper limits of joy, if there are any. Instead, more driving rain, testing the extremes of misery, and how to live there, and smile. Then they built this school along the road I'm walking, and changed everything. I started the fire with pages from a ratty dictionary found on the floor. It wasn't easy.

You think my doing this is crass, and disrespectful of a country landmark. It is, but not absolutely: I swept clean this entranceway before settling in. It needed it. The doors and windows are already gone, and the floor of the main room next to me has rotted and sunk and received an unwelcoming mix of lath and plaster and pigeon shit. If anything I've set back the processes of dilapidation with my off-the-beat occupation.

○

The roads here kill redbelly snakes.

September 20: The wind carries on, from out of the north. Walking into it two days now, and with the clouds and flocks of birds hurtling south, it seems the earth is rolling north with me.

They never tell you about the swallows. Ours could be as celebrated as Capistrano's, if we had as lilting a name. Walking, I've been surrounded by flocks of them, as far as my good eyes can see their tiny forms, as if the whole country hosted them. They are silent, foraging low over stubble fields and meadows alike, and flying upwind so to look down is to feel awash in a great gulf stream of dark little birds. Whether they are migrants or locals they will be leaving soon, but with a flourish that will lure me back to see them again someday.

September 21: I can't help it if swallows and other birds keep appearing in this account. (Foxes, my familiar, would have also recurred, but they've been another secret I've kept.) Birds because they are impossible to ignore: vocal and mobile and fairly abundant. And they are just another of the elements of this region. I would have done well to have composed these pages as a series of sketches, with a page or two for each element, from the stars on down to my feet, bringing the scattered elements together as a portrait, a sort of primer for the plains. And in the process elevating each without artifice as an essential feature of the world, and of the other elements:

night stars earth fog dew sun clouds wind shadow rain mud dust shale spring lake evening waves wheatgrass sage grouse plum owl gopher swallow snake sand and turtle and cottonwood creeks

They are the many ways into the world, as introductions, separable as each is separate: only long enough to see how they fit together:

Earth is air and water. Night turns them to fog, then dew, and the sun dissolves these in the same order. The wind is from the sun, and sends cloud shadows over everything that follows: hills of grass and trees. Rain is something in-between, turns shale dust to mud, spring lakes, waves, wheatgrass, sage and grouse.

I am well practiced at separating them, charmed by their names, so now I'm relearning, trying to say their names with one breath.

They are inevitabilities. Consider evening, the *feel* of evening. And morning, and their being so different. Imagine hating all that.

These elements are not all benign. A whole other list could be compiled, and integrated with the first, to show the earth as an unpleasant or unhealthy place: windy, cold, hot, muddy, dusty, prickly, burred, *spined.* Biting, stinging. *Teethed and coming.*

September 22: I should be placing the clouds at your feet. Instead so often here I've arrived at some fine place or moment and not described it, or only briefly related how fine it was. Because I've noted its existence and wish to say no more. I might not do it well enough, or too well and you'll be content with my account and hear only my words when finally you experience it. No matter how pure I feel or well I do I think that I'm stealing some magic from the world, and selling it to you, and spoiling it.

But some spirit breathes through me when I do this, something I speak for. In a fluent intermingling of thought and matter I'm running my brain through things and distilling their essence, the essence of thought. And is their elegance necessary to my thinking or only a creation of it?

Thinking about these places and how they connect has me burrowing through the language searching for words, finding old words nearly forgotten with the places—I feel as though I'm exploring the language through the landscape. And not at all imposing a language on the land. So I really shouldn't complain about this writing, this wording, as long as the places come first, and the thoughts are well grounded.

I awake each day and begin a game of concentration, of remembrance and composition. I would like to learn to experience it without forgetting, and remember without losing track. Track it without guiding it, guide without taming, and when I get lost find my way back.

○

Passing through a town I caught the headlined news of an historic arms treaty being signed. We find ourselves writing sentences unimagined only a week before. Maybe I should leave more often. And can I take some credit for the peace in my own heart?

<u>September 23:</u> The days passed in places so flowered and softly grassed it hurts to walk. Only by this intimate transit can I feel the costs involved in travel, both the pain I feel and the pain I cause. It may be too much trouble for some, caring so much for such little things. But I relish the challenge that I pose, delving feet first through these intricacies and trying to eliminate the least of my trespasses, until a footfall is too much.

Look what we have done with our feet:

stand
stare
state
stay

○

This keeps suggesting its own ending, in the balance of it, one day into autumn with bluebirds reappearing, southbound on this side of their orbit; in the breakdowns and the aching body parts; and by the particular places suffering from my lack of attention as I attend to ranges wider than I could ever much affect.

A week ago I was in a car riding with a farmer and a self-proclaimed dirty old man. They returning from Aberdeen with a TV stop at Stratford for beer. Waiting outside the bar I am when the bus from Warner drops off the town's grade-schoolers. Then we're driving again, drinkers rolling through a group of kids. A girl lingers, she is running and we are catching up. Dirty old man says, "Look out for that one, she might jump across." But I knew she wouldn't, I'd watched her all the way, and seen her once leaping for the sake of leaping over some spot only she could see on the ground. She knew about us. We were beside her on my side, she glanced our way and through the hair blown across her face I could see: indifference, accusation. Adults in cars. We didn't count. She looked back to her leaping.

○

When I started I imagined so much more that I would say and do. But then the imagining was effortless. *A wind in your mind that curls around on itself.* What was it I forgot to say? It can wait. *Our bad ideas like sidewalks crack.* So much that I was going to put before you. *Turn welcome mats around to welcome you outdoors.* Now I would be gladder to shut up, to sputter into reverent silence: the silence that was here before I began. I've told too many secrets already.

There's nothing to be done
    (empty your hands)

nowhere to go
    (hoist the world onto your back)

I don't know what to tell you
    (may words fail you)

Is this the side I fall on?

    save the spirit
    break the letter

A book that sets out to be a final book has a little explaining to do. It would be hypocrisy to set myself against books and all mediated experience and then join right in. Even though I do pose the problem from the start (I will fail if you keep reading) and make the book a work of immediacy, teaching of it, the book's existence refutes its message: a page is a wonderful thing to waste. With hope that hypocrisy may be canceled by discussing itself I choose paper *once and for all* to argue against paper and the many devices of our recording culture. A book merely celebrating earth would be hypocrisy.

So what are we to make of this dissonance: I wanted you to rediscover the earth, so I wrote a book. Contrarily, with a process that takes us both away from the subject I invite you to experience that subject. And the better I am at my task of writing the more likely it is you will be kept to yours, of reading. The better I am at rendering true the world the more you may be diverted from it, satisfied and even preferring my version, other versions, *versions.* And you miss the world in reading about it.

As if this was the worst way to miss the world. Books aren't the worst of all the seductive media—not necessarily about the earth's magnificence!—attracting us away from the real thing.

Writing and reading teach us about having imaginary worlds before us, with our focus far removed from what they are about: the world about the world. But everything can't be about something else; some things must be about themselves. Or else it becomes emptier, ever less substantial the farther we go into mediated experience until it should suggest its own ending: the original was superior to any of the copies. Better a real fox.

Farther and farther we go from our lives being about anything that ever really happened, and we may as well be lying in a meadow daydreaming. And I cannot decide if it is better, for real foxes, that so many are turned away from them, as I myself have been. (It is not too late to sound a thought that occurred time and again in my travels: *where is everybody?*—from having such splendor all to myself.) The turning away leaves foxes alone, but it also bulldozes and buries, smothers in paper and allows forgetting.

Reader, you doubt that forgetting could have so much to do with change in the world. Then try to remember or imagine elements of the world, and ways of being in it, that you never knew. *Change, forgetting, change.* And the change I write of is less in the way of things suddenly appearing than of their gradually fading away. Elements of the world already unnoticed and unspoken; small, perhaps, and secretive. Underground. Nocturnal. The forgetting is easier as we lose those elements, and the losing is easier as we forget they even exist. Which comes first? What are the ways out of this spiral?

One sweet day in June I realized with a flash that my goal with this book is to have more people hearing more pipits. It's that simple. But it's their task as much as mine, and as much a matter of giving the pipits more space as it is getting people out in that space.

Pipits are sparrow-sized birds that nest in native prairie from the Dakotas on north and west into Canada. Pedestrian birds, drab and streaked like the grass, they especially would go unnoticed if not for their song: bright ringing tones sounded from high in a spiraling courtship flight—but ventriloqual so the sound seems to be right beside you. Its song is everything the poets have claimed for the skylarks of Europe. So if pipit song can't do it, can't invite and reconnect you to the earth—the empty sky will have to do.

This book may have failed as an act of invitation, reconnection, and preserving what passes. May that failure not weaken the themes at its heart: preserving the earth and experiencing it, directly, and each for the other: preserving earth to experience it, and the experience awakening the urge to preserve. If pipits had passed before I'd heard their song—

If I am trying to impress you with a world passing away before you even knew it was there, why should I persist in the futility of that? Better that I should set my talents to easing the loss and hastening the forgetting. A life lived in cars and buildings I should celebrate, life less in-the-body. I should explore and adapt to a landscape shaped by and for machines. It must be a measure of my hope that I do not.

At heart I believe the earth will be saved not by people saving it as much as by people loving it. So my task is doubly in doubt before I begin: teaching a love that can't be taught, to those who aren't listening.

What can't be taught:

You must make your own intimate acquaintance with this world.

You can't *imagine* it, and certainly none can do it for you, least of all such words. But I think you'll recognize it when some dazzling moment reminds you—after a snowfall, a ray of light— Next time let it carry you with it in a self enriching cycle of understanding, appreciation, and understanding. —Because it exists at least with your awareness, not just in front of you. It leads you into and through a landscape so completely and well your mind could be located anywhere within. It takes time, and there will be bungling along the way, some you never know about. There are no shortcuts. It can be learned but not taught.

to those who aren't listening:

The readers I would address aren't reading this, not even close. They live lives far removed from anything I understand and love and am trying to convey. They like it that way, living with little reference to the earth, surrounding and devouring the world any writer, in a lifetime, only begins to love. Living lives that, from books to war movies to war, would be better suited for a space station and seem bent on turning earth into one. This is the part hardest to accept. But it gets worse: not only are people seduced away from the natural world, there is also ever-less of it to attract them back should they be willing to be so moved, and less of it for writers to refer to in their efforts to reintroduce readers.

It gets to be a losing cause, a self-defeating cycle that one enters at some risk: to attract the reader without seducing you, and to transcribe the world without further papering it over.

For once the earth has been papered over with our stories, what will our stories be about? Are we making such legends on earth as will leave only a legendary earth as our setting? The earth is consumed to feed spectators watching an imaginary world, and so much of the real world is gone to support our fictional one. Half acting, half watching; all eating. How long can the earth support our essential lives, much less our reruns?

A thousand metaphors won't feed you. Perhaps it is a human trait, to prefer and even addict to a storied world. And maybe it makes no difference to our minds or to the earth if we are immersed in a fabricated world. But I don't think we can live there for long. We don't now, although some of us may live by propagating fictions.

If the earth had gone merely to meet our needs I would have much less of an argument. To the extent that it has gone to satisfy what we have and do beyond our needs I have an argument, which gets serious when that satisfaction means choking off the earth that gives the satisfaction meaning and makes survival possible. For when the earth reaches the state of being smothered in our grasp surely the first to go will have to be our fabricated lives, the farthest from necessity? Giving them up because they steal from our real lives? When we reach the point of our stories consuming their subject something will have to give. (Yet the process is so slow and roundabout we strain to see the direct connection. No one cuts a tree for the pencil and paper to tell its life history, or pours a field into a stone monument.) We can't have both: we begin to lose the stories because they are being told. As if we could live in a world with all stories and no things.

As it is I have no argument without first subtracting myself. For I have been there, so remote from need as to forget it, fully enrolled in the modern curriculum of mediated, human-centered, this-could-be-any-room-anywhere experience. The argument is for *me* to define necessity, recognize what's beyond that as freedom, and choose my first steps.

And if anything, the journal that precedes chronicles the difficulties in taking such steps as much as it celebrates the rewards. It says, "no compromise" then proceeds to discover the compromises along the way: a little less joy, say, for a little less pain. "I don't get far" emerged early as a theme, as my journey became a smooth flow through neither space or time. The journal entries show it and are more of a "selected notes from a journal" to hide the disruptions, the compromises.

The farther you've come from the earth, from immediate and reverent connection with it, the more stuff you'll have to slog through to get back. You can't do it all at once. But I'm not asking you to *get there now*; only turn in that direction. And keep it. If what I say has any truth you may remember it along the way.

You will protest that the turning was away from the harshness of the world, its very heaviness, the endless rounds of moons and years, and all the everyday elements that make life on earth unpleasant, difficult, dangerous. Night. Winter. And this account to be true has emphasized wind, rain, mud, drought, insects, snakes, wind—interspersed with whole days, in series, of the most beneficent calm—itself another extreme. What corrects, what makes up for these givens?

Do you know the world I am talking about? Did you ever? Or have you turned so far so long from earth you have no experience or memory of the harshness you were escaping? And in escaping the hard part you missed the joy, then devalued it? Somehow this free, spectacular scene became commonplace. For being uneventful? Boring, forgotten, and now unknown. Large truths go unworded. But the unknown can't be ordinary, and we've come full circle, to where the world can be rediscovered for being new and unknown. Just in time.

I don't know in what order these words should appear, or if they should appear. The words come through me, blameless the both of us, and unselfconscious. Whether or not to utter them is my conscious choice but even when I do I still feel innocent, the words harmless nothings until acted upon. Unlike the rivers you can always change their sign. Reading them would be the first act but it's not much without remembrance. We maintain our innocence until that point. Innocence is not the word for this, it's more like caprice: the lesson in these words appearing is that they could be others, or otherwise.

I must put certain words before you. I am a creature of them as much as you are. These ideas I've been carrying around with me for years I want to put out here and be done with—shared! the first time for you!—and go on to others. (May these produce others.) I'm not really interested in writing so I've lured you into this book long and well enough to convince you to stop reading, so I can stop writing. This might surprise some who think writers are interested only in words, when it's actually the world we want to get close to, not its names. The world is too definite for words so vague. It's like seeking vision through blindness, and one should try another sense.

Nothing is felt as words. But nothing felt is kept without them. Use the right words and the whole body believes them. They disappear in the telling, surpassed by their message: ideas that good. The words evaporate behind us as they leave us with the feeling. We're walking a line between word and message, symbol and meaning. Each exists at the expense of the other—if one's better one's poorer—yet wouldn't exist without the other. The words get in the way of the feelings, or else the feelings come to regulate the body before the body has words to defend itself. Words get in the way, writing is not living, everything stops for writing until all there is to write about is one's writing. To write much and observe little. All the days I lost to produce a record of other days, these days.

Too busy living to write: too many times I've thought this through without writing it down, preferring the original, happy with the thought—get your own—so long I thought this through without writing until one night before sleep I dreamed the book was done, I felt so sure, and more than that: it was read. And more than that: understood. Believed. And more than that: by many.

This book is an invitation to wandering in the world and in the mind. If the writing was any good it would send you outside at any hour. When it's less than that it may at least make you slam the book shut and be shy about opening others. In between, if I've served the words well they will serve the earth well, if the earth is worth serving.

The journal did serve as an act of remembrance, through my enhanced memory of these times and places. Although the journal is brief the journey was not: I resolve to do it as much as I can wherever I am: travel or stay, on foot, outside, and realize how much I *lived* there.

NOTES

Page

i *True:* If the title seems ostentatious, think of it as the carpenter's sense of the word, as a verb. With a period after, it's the first sentence of the book, an imperative.

iii *Notes from journeys:* The map sections on the next two pages enclose most of the areas in which I traveled. (They are from the USGS Shaded Relief map of South Dakota.) The maps illustrate well many of the physical features I visited or discuss at length here. Showing the routes I took clutters the map excessively; tracing my routes exactly isn't necessary to the reading. And it would leave little for you to puzzle together on your own. Other sites mentioned, such as towns, can be found on other maps of South Dakota.

I had two home bases for these jaunts, just east of the Black Hills and in Faulk County, the latter from July on. (July was devoted to harvest.) By far the greatest part of my time was spent on public land and ways, as I invariably aimed for public lands, state or federal, via section lines and roads. This was hardly possible throughout, so whenever I crossed private land I tried to ask somebody if it was okay. They always seemed more charmed than alarmed by my presence. If I trespassed it was not done maliciously, I took nothing, and left little more than a patch of matted grass to mark my passing.

The greatest daily concern is, of all things, for stampeding cattle. As other creatures do they seem unaccustomed to the sight of a human passing on foot. (But drive by slowly in a pickup truck and they're likely to approach you, expecting feed or something.) Several times I took great detours to avoid herds of cattle. Even then they do what they want: a couple herds took off running when I rolled by, as proper as could be, on a public road.

For all my care I can hardly recommend that this experiment be widely repeated. It sounds awful, the prospect of many people out stealing through the land, camping and carrying on. It punches a great hole in this book. Except there was little danger of such a mass exodus happening. I had these places all to myself, and would again; even the public lands. There is a lot of space for a person walking. I can look across the creek from my place to where I first set out and be reasonably sure that in the past three years only one person has walked there. A few have driven, checking livestock or hunting. I've also bicycled through.

This prospect of a mass exodus, contrasted with the current reality of *no* exodus, in neither mass nor driblet, raises some important questions. There is no danger, yet, of this place being loved to death. There was a time not long ago when people were out in the world

LAWRENCE
PENNINGTON
CUSTER
FALL RIVER
Crow Peak
Bear Butte
Oyster Mtn
Sturgis
Deadwood
Bear Den Mtn
Deadman Mtn
4943
Terry Peak
Deer Mtn
Limestone Plateau
Spearfish Creek
Bear Butte Creek
Spring Cr
Alkali Creek
Belle Fourche River
Dry Elm Cr
Elm
Hay Creek
Bull Creek
Eightmile
Divide
2717
Costello Point
3194
Antelope Cr
Morris Cr
Elk Creek
Crystal Mtn
6421
Crooks Tower
South Fk
White Tail Peak
Green Mtn
Norris Peak
RAPID CITY
Boxelder Creek
Rapid Creek
Crows Nest Peak
Pactola Reservoir
5922
Scruton Mtn
Victoria
Old Baldy Peak
6779
Hat Mtn
Ditch Cr
Smith Mtn
Cobbler Knob
Thompson Butte
3457
Railroad Buttes
Spring Creek
Dipping Vat Draw
Timber
Kube
5655
Summit Peak
5725
Mount Rushmore
Harney Peak
Bear Mtn
Signal Hill
Dead Horse Flats
Surveyors Hill
Custer
Mt Coolidge
6023
Grace Coolidge Cr
Battle Creek
Red Shirt Cr
Schenk Can
Hell Canyon
6166
South Fork
French Creek
Cheyenne
Cottonwood Creek
Lame Johnny Cr
Pilger Mtn
4788
Beaver Creek
Harrison Flat
Flat
Black Canyon
Squaw Humper Table
Cedar Creek
Red Shirt
East Fk
West Fk
Willow Cr
Hot Springs
Canyon
Red
Parker Peak
Roundtop Hill
Angostura Reservoir
Flattop Mtn
Tepee Mtn
Hay Canyon Butte
3460
Horsehead
N Fk
S Fk
Blacktail
Cottonwood Cr
River
Plum Cr
Ash Cr
4005
Plains Cr
Hat Cr
Beaver Creek
Creek
White River
Slim Butte
3223
SHA
White

HAAKON
JACKSON
WASHABAUGH
BENNETT
MILESVILLE
FLAT
Hudson Flat
Stony Butte Draw
Davidson Flat
Timber Cr
Pine Cr
Badlands Cr
Poverty Pond
Squaw Cr
Mixes Food Cr
Deep Creek
Ash Creek
Bridger Creek
Snake Creek
East Fork
Grindstone Butte
Mexican Creek
Grindstone Cr
Medicine Creek
Buzzard Creek
Mitchell Creek
North Fork
Waggoner Lake
Philip
Bad River
Cedar Butte
2889
Cedar Cr
Cottonwood Creek
Crooked Creek
South Fork
Bad
Creek
Indian Cr
Raiders Hills
Round Hill
South
White Willow Creek
Brady Cr
West Fork
South Fork
3255
Kadoka
Runs-Close
Horseshoe Butte
Red Stone Cr
Cottonwood Creek
Long Cr
Eagle Nest Creek
Grayson Cr
Eagle Butte
Medicine Root Creek
Porcupine
Eagle Nest Butte
Buzzard Butte
Snake Butte
No Flesh Cr
American Horse Creek
Creek
Spring Cr
Porcupine Butte
Martin
South
Alkali Lake
3680
3530
Fantom Lake

WALWORTH
EDMUNDS
POTTER
FAULK
Mound City
Selby
Ipswich
Leola
Gettysburg
Faulkton
Onida
Alkali Lake
Richmond Lake
Lords Lake
Lake Parmley
North Scatterwood Lake
Spring Lake
Swan Lake
Blue Blanket Lake
Molstad Lake
Hiddenwood Cr
Trail City RR Lake
Clark Lake
Dry Lake
Stone Lake
Rice Lake
Thomas Lake
Rezac Lake
Cottonwood Lake
Twin Lakes
Artichoke Butte
Skully Buttes
Virgin Creek
Snake Creek
Foot Creek
Campbell Cr
Medicine Cr
North Wolf Creek
Matter Cr
Shaefer
South Fork
1850
1925
1750
2015
1960
2010
2090

HYDE
HAND
HUGHES
BUFFALO
JERAUL
LYMAN
BRULE
AUROR
Highmore
Miller
Pierre
Fort Pierre
MISSOURI
RIVER
Wessington Springs
Gannvalley
Kennebec
Chamberlain
Murdo
White Clay Butte
White River
Spring Lake
Crow Lake
Bedashosha Lake
Nail Creek Lake
Mud Lake
Silver Lake
Red Lake
White Lake
Wilmarth Lake
Platte Lake
Crystal Lake
FORT RANDALL
Medicine
Smith
Cain
Anderson Ridge
Willow
War Cr
Herd Camp Cr
North Fork
Chapelle Creek
South Chapelle Cr
South Fork
Campbell
Soldier Cr
Little Elm Cr
West Fork
Crow Creek
Big Creek
Bad Cr
Heap Lake
Mission Cr
Cottonwood Creek
Dog Ear
Old Lodge
Hunter Cr
Nelson Cr
Elm Cr
Platte Creek
East Fork
2210
2235
2004

more than they are today. And was the world more alive then? Or being slaughtered right and left? If the world is less alive now, is it in part from our turning away? If so, we can turn towards it, we need to, and the world can become wilder because of, not in spite of, us.

And anyway I embrace the challenge these questions force, of living as lightly as possible; lightness for its own sake.

I carried with me the minimum necessary supplies: a lightweight two-person tent, sleeping bag, rain pants and jacket, three shirts, one pair of pants, a bird book, binoculars, camera and microcassette recorder. For water I had a Katadyn filter, which allowed me to drink almost any water. For food I had venison jerky, rice, bulgur, nuts and dried fruits. The rice and bulgur were cooked at night with some home-grown dried vegetables, along with whatever I gathered from the land. Next morning I added a little brown sugar to the leftovers for breakfast: glorified rice. I did not fish or trap or hunt. Plants I gathered included asparagus, thistle stems, cacti, mushrooms, chokecherries, plums—the last two were plentiful by August and September. I had boxes of the dried mixtures sent ahead general delivery to post offices I would stop at, knowing that the small towns I would be passing through with their little stores and cafes would offer narrow choices for traveling provisions. I did "forage and gather" in some, though.

By June on the plains I'd left my sleeping bag at home, sleeping in the tent with just a sheet and lightweight long underwear to keep me warm. They were always sufficient.

The water filter was indispensable for making any water potable, by filtering out bacteria and parasites. There is no better feeling than walking thirsty up to a body of water and knowing you can drink. Still, the filter didn't keep out the water's flavor, so I carried herb teas to steep in the water to mask the flavor. Nor did it keep out the minerals, smaller than bacteria and just as effective, giving me farts and diarrhea no matter what I tried. Especially west-river, where the people I visited with along the way knew all too well the water situation, stressing that *they* had good water—usually brought in from elsewhere. One man pointed out what I'd already learned, that the well water was "clear and cold, the best you ever tasted, but oh it makes you sick." One and all, they couldn't quite use the word diarrhea, perhaps out of kindness for me standing there downwind with my stomach gurgling.

As the summer dried the waters away the journey became more than anything the search for water. Good water is a problem across the state, and always has been, although it is getting better with the building of water projects from Missouri River reservoirs. So I was often obliged to approach farmhouses for water, and just as often apologetic when the residents reached for a jug by the sink—not wanting to deplete their hand-carried supply.

This search gave me many opportunities to visit with people along the way, and two trends emerged. There were several men who expressed envy to me, saying words to the effect, "you're doing what every man would like to do." *Man* may be the key word here, because the women were much more skeptical, and exemplified by a woman who said, "I don't envy you your life." (And the way she said it, suddenly I didn't either.)

The microcassette recorder was indispensable, the closest thing to a thought recorder yet invented. It allowed me to take notes in stride, hands free, on what I was seeing or thinking. I could also record the sounds around me, with variable clarity. Listening to the tapes later helped me to recreate the ambiance of the places I'd been, sometimes surprising me with the "background" sounds I'd recorded—birds, wind, frogs and crickets, my footsteps on dry rocks or sloshing through water.

The way the travels were arranged, from west to east of the Missouri River, turns out to be an appropriate travel through time. West-river is an older landscape and its past reaches into the present fairly well intact. East-river is not only of more recent creation, since the retreat of the last glacier, it is also more extensively sundered from its past by conversion to agriculture. Also, the modes of travel I used—mostly hiking west-river while biking on the east side—these modes are fitting because there's less to experience among the wheatfields, cornfields, stubble and fallow east-river, so you need to go faster to cover more ground and strain out the finer things.

This two-sided river, the Missouri, should be conspicuous by its absence from this account. In early September I was aiming for it. I'd just left the road and was rolling across country, nearing the shore when my bike's derailleur broke hopelessly. Since I had no replacement I had a choice of hitching to Aberdeen for repairs or pushing the bike along the river twenty miles to the next road. I went for repairs, and didn't return to the river.

I'd thought I might write about the river by saying I was going down to the river, the river Missouri, and then leave the page blank. "The blank page of forget," for the river drowned by dams through much of the Dakotas. A more profound example of change and forgetting is unlikely to be found in this state. Plowing of the prairie is profound, but it's been gradual, and done by thousands of individuals. The damming was virtually instantaneous, and was the decision, ultimately, of a couple hundred people in the U.S. Congress. History shows that most of the people in the state stood quietly by, said nothing to stop it, and did little to commemorate the river before it drowned. There was not even a requiem. Apparently no one was very much bothered by taking a million-years-old river and plugging it overnight (the dambuilders worked day and night). Who sat by the river and watched the waters go still? Who counted the animals fleeing or drowned? Who cared about the animals returning to a strange new lake, animals lost and disconcerted, hungry, sick, and failing? Did anyone cry?

This is the feeling of before and after. All of us born too late to stop the dams have to accept the reservoirs. We'll never get to know this now-legendary river.

But the river is still very much alive, if unrecognizably changed, and probably more in control of its destiny than the dam-tenders would admit. It still has a strong flow through the reservoirs, which aren't just stagnant pools. The river cuts sharp cliffs into the bank on one side of a curve while leaving a flat shore on the other bank, just as it always has. When the reservoirs are full of water their waves erode both shores, which helps to fill the reservoirs and shorten their lifespan. Eventually the water level goes down, as it has the past few years, and the shale shore turns to dust, blowing into the water in another reservoir-filling process. When high water returns the reservoirs have less capacity, or else the same volume of water is forced higher on the shore, causing more erosion, more filling. . . .

The alternating water level is producing dammed marshes in most of the river's tributaries, small or large. Cottonwoods, willows, and grasses are sprouting along the shore, especially far upstream from the dams. When the waters rise again this vegetation may be fatally drowned, but in the process it provides habitat for fish and waterfowl while catching suspended sediments—more filling.

So the drowned river will revive itself, although not as before. Its great history deserves a blank page to commemorate its passing, but its great power is already writing the next pages with an exciting new version.

⊙

Some of the "notes" included here are actually from letters and postcards sent to friends and later recovered and used, sometimes in their entirety, herein. A sample, from March:

hello sister,

here are some copies of pages from a great book by Kenneth patchen: hallelua anyway. i would love to see the originals, in multi-color. (the book is in brown tones) he has many other books - check them out

see how easy it is to send letters?. actually, i'd feel kinda cheap if i left it at that - or this. or this. this?

but as you can see i kept writing. but what did i write? this? can you trust me to the end of this sentence

now packing to leave tomorrow. blizzard at my back, i hope - it would be so dramatic, so real, so cold. but would it sell? who would believe i'd be so daring, or so dumb? nah, i'll be holed up in a riverside juniper wi' my friends the owl + the fox + the grouse. telling tales we will be.

i can't wait. won't.

no-action requires no knowledge and allows

all-learning

the moon flies high this year
don't miss it

michael

v *About head high:* A phrase lost in my personal antiquity. It has something to do with thinking better on my feet, the view from there, and in walking the way the near ground bobs against the horizon. Or consider how many photographs are taken from that position.

The earth warms: Adopted for this chapter in early 1990 when I heard a radio report about the prospects for South Dakota's new video lottery through the summer: "When the earth warms and people spend more time outdoors. . ." Such a splendid phrase, used in an otherwise base economic analysis.

The symbol for seeing: From the Badlands National Park map symbol for scenic view.

Killdeer brother: I was taught that in Lakota, the language of the land I walked through, one of the words for killdeer is the same as the word for brother: tiblǒ. Both languages claim to imitate the bird's call in naming the bird. Which comes closer? And what if I'd called the chapter "Brother killdeer?"

rock problems: Rock or boulder problems are what climbers (mountaineers) call their routes, dreamed or realized, up a rock. So there are none of these in Faulk County, unless you consider grain elevators, spillways, the courthouse—

Immortality changes everything: An elaboration of the saying "Prayer changes things."

more at stand: The origin, and alternate title, for the poem on page 74. See a dictionary for further explanation.

5 *a predicted blizzard:* Blizzards are open-plains weather, strong winds driving heavy snow, zero visibility sometimes lasting two days and two nights. Thus my journey already threatened, or promised, drama, danger, an early end.

a rich pastel: As in *paste.*

a conventional map: from such a map you could have guessed that I would collect cacti on private land (overgrazed), and gumbo on public land (National Grasslands often being relegated to the poorest soils and/or topography). The condition of the range on the private lands mentioned has been much improved by the caretakers in the three years since.

6 *And below:* If the river valley is a furrow then in cross-section it is a V, and that is figuratively how the life above it collects there and disperses therefrom. The waters, too, of course, and they diffuse again rather like a V below ground, mirroring the one above and supporting a whole other zone of life there—invertebrates, mostly, both permanent

residents and tenants eventually metamorphosing away.

the blue light in snow: Snow absorbs the red side of light first, so the blue light goes in farther until it's the only light left. But you have to get inside to see it.

8 *top of their heads:* prairie dogs, rabbits, gophers. . . .

10 *heaven of rain:* This applies at least for a continental climate like that of the Great Plains, rain-shadowed by the Rocky Mountains.

12 *the days accelerate:* Actually, at any point the run-off can be stalled by colder weather. But once the water starts to flow we feel the pull of inevitability, and that certain days have passed irrevocably. The inevitable is not all kind—it's flooding, after all, too late to prepare for.

and that sound: of falling water.

15 *pronghorn. . . antelope:* The latter is the common name but we're supposed to learn the former, so I'll help by using it throughout. Which means I'll have to tell this story now: I'd thought pronghorns were shy, and it'd been my experience to have seen them usually running away. So to have this one approach as close as it did, and to have others do so in days to come—I had to rethink their behavior, and mine, and was soon attributing it to my uniformly sandy-colored clothes—"my antelope clothes" I called them. I carried and wore them throughout the summer.

(I see now I know next to nothing about the pronghorn, if it's true that "thirty-one separate behavior patterns, along with a variety of vocalizations, have been described for them."—Clark & Stromberg, *Mammals in Wyoming,* 1987.)

16 *old, old Hills:* "the Hills", whenever capitalized, will refer to the Black Hills.

dammed upstream: Angostura Dam.

walking wood sampler: It's a long story, but back in March I'd accidently poked myself in the cheek with a pine bough and still had a piece lodged there, thinking/hoping it was scar tissue.

17 *the August side:* a mostly astronomical calculation, April and August being similar in the length of their days but not in their average temperatures.

always posing: In the spirit of this chapter, yes, they are photogenic.

18 *buffalo wallows:* Well, the thought has charm, and there might be something to it. But there are more biting insects than breed in water. And for those that do, the bison provide plenty of breeding holes

simply by their legs punching holes in any mud: clay vessels holding water long after even a little rain.

19 *There are two sides:* The circumstance involved in one creek flowing north while the other faces south should not be underestimated. If *you* were to face south all the time, and all your waterfall ledges expose cliffs fully to the sun while their counterparts to the north throw that much more shade—the extremes suggest the advantage in turning away even slightly from the sun in this climate and latitude. It shows in the vegetation of the two valleys. I found an even more striking example on May 6: a formation eroded to a grass-capped pillar about ten feet high, wedge-shaped with one of the sides facing southeast. That side was barren of vegetation, not least for being vertical, while the north side actually had moss growing on it. I could step one step either way and see the principle irrefutably demonstrated.

where the water escapes: With a pattern so subtle I followed one down as it curved south, I thought, leading me to an easy way down, I thought, until the subtleties added up to a definite northward flow.

20 *buck chasing a doe:* Actually, I couldn't confirm the sex of the front-runner.

21 *many will come:* Which is about all I could remember verbatim. It's Matthew 8:11. (These born-again people seem to quote the Old Testament exclusively.) Other favorites: "Do not heap up empty phrases" (Matthew 6:7) and the one about having faith to move mountains (Matthew 21:21)—at least it sets a direction.

22 *precious. . .on any scale:* To the scale of this county maybe not, but in the state certainly, the globe more so, the universe exquisitely so; today, yes, one hundred years past, perhaps not.

nothing need be done: after Gary Snyder: "Knowing that nothing need be done, is where we begin to move from." (From *Turtle Island*, p. 102.)

23 *our daily snake:* And then get it over with. The rattlesnakes keep us on our toes even when we're off our feet; they keep us off our feet. (Yet another excuse, at least in summertime, for staying home, on the pavement, in the car). Walking you expect with every step to meet a snake, but actually in the average day only one such step will occur, so each day becomes something of a wait—pacing—for that day's snake. The next day brought me three rattlesnakes, after the rain had begun. From my notes:

I found three vipers curled by their holes, cooled asleep. Their scales were washed and bright—pretty, the diamonds, but not enough to hold.

24 *I haven't moved:* I wonder if you can get carried away with this idea. Here's a journal entry from this day that extends the idea while discussing a related one:

The hitchhiking from west of Interior, although necessary—I was about out of food—was not good. I feel dislocated, a loss of the continuity that is really necessary when easing into a strange land. Not that rolling the earth at 60 mph is being questioned, here. (Now there's an image: we're not moving, not going anywhere, just staying in our cars, spinning the wheels and rolling the globe.) Continuity between familiar points could be kept at those rates. . . But here I have jumped to a new valley so different from the Cheyenne, and I need that continuity to make sense of the differences. First, the trees are bigger, healthier, more leafed-out. Many more willows and young trees. On the Cheyenne young trees are rare, willows uncommon, the cottonwoods large-trunked but gnarled and broken, sprouty. As if someone had suddenly plugged that river upstream about fifty years ago. I shouldn't be too hasty in blaming the dam; after all I've taken only a small sample of a very different river (whole 'nother watershed, narrower streambed, different ownership patterns), and done so nearly four very warm days since I was at this latitude on the Cheyenne. The trees there may be as leafed-out by now. . . . Some already were when I was there. But most of them had that look of, "yeah, it's spring, and we're excited, but actually we're going to die back a little more this year."

The coyote: See page 9.

27 *eating red, seeing red:* Reds are from carotenoids, pigments found in plants and animals and convertible to vitamin A, which aids vision. From my notes:

The plants distill it from earth and sky. With it they speak to birds and butterflies (winged flowers, flower wings). And these among themselves: a simple yes or no will do; come close, stay away. And to me: the blackbird's raised epaulet signaling "red-winged". It's all very simple from the molecule's point of view, now lodged in rock, now root, now squirrel hair.

a muddy May: The woods by the springs were horribly trampled by cattle, all over the hillside above it and down on the outwash below.

only two deer: By contrast, I'd seen about six a day of both species since April 26, whether on private or public land.

Everyone knows: Because I'd heard it said several times that the game is "all hunted out" on the reservations. Just five days earlier, in Interior, I'd heard it again. I didn't *want* to believe it, and had trouble with the logic: if the game's all hunted out, what is there to hunt?

28 *the scene repeated:* the "neighbor" had reported that the Tribe's prairie dog extermination campaign had just reached this valley before the past winter. As I write this (Jan. '91), plans are being made to mine this

Page

and several other valleys for zeolite, a mineral to be sold as a fertilizer component and for chicken coop litter.

unbroken and unspoiled: When broken land has become the rule we have to use the negative term to describe the original.

29 *beyond the river:* The Missouri.

on different planets: As this narrative begins to swallow its tail . . .

South Dakota in 1973: If you recall the "Wounded Knee uprising."

the snowblind moon: I swear I just now learned this, that March was called the snowblind moon (month) by the Sioux people. Although history will note, if it bothers, that I probably learned it eight years earlier, in a Lakota language class at USD. The point being that in March when I was worried about going snowblind I was rediscovering it for myself. March with its glazed snow, the sun to higher air, and perhaps the human urge to travel south to meet spring on its way.

wasicu: Pronounced wa-she'chu, it interprets as "one who takes the fat."

30 *two puffballs: Lycoperdon* fungi, which is to say, rain three days ago. Their spore-filled remains persist long after maturation, and kicking them releases a brown smoke of spores.

this hunger: The original version read, "This hunger, that rain, this freedom . . .", referring to the rain three days before.

33 *in a cemetery:* Much of my note-taking was with a microcassette recorder, which allowed me to record my thoughts on the go. Even then I didn't keep track all that well, except for bird and natural history observations. It's not my nature or habit to think out loud. So I often found myself catching up after a couple-three days, as on this night. (One way to "write" in the dark.) Soon after I turned on the recorder a Venus-bright meteor flashed on my right, producing an audible, recorded gasp and sigh. From there I went into an intense exploration of the ideas in "Killdeer brother"—probably at greater length than I do here—*long past the time the tape reached its end.* I was devastated, realizing I'd lost some irreplaceable, particular wordings. It got worse: recovering what I'd lost meant leaving the train of thought where I was, backing up to hear what I'd recorded and what not, then filling in the lost parts up to where I'd backed up. And then much of it was garbled, me eating and talking and rustling food bags—grace with every bite, indeed.

angels or birds: I can explain this hallucination. I'd heard snipes winnowing several times before; it really is an unforgettable sound. But this time the sound was distorted, carrying to me as ripples in the wind. It was just how I'd imagine angel voices to be. If this is a confession then it is only to imagining spirit in the world. (If there is spirit in the world the snipe will surpass.) And I'd been prepped: I'd met a psychic the year before, who told me I'm an old soul, soon to be contacted by spirits, and when it happened I would laugh—"That's me!" So let's just say it was easy to imagine, all the while realizing ever more it was a snipe. A delicious moment there, holding the belief and the contradictory knowledge in my mind, with a real let-down when the knowledge came to rule.

a fossil print: Pure conjecture at the time, I've since learned that it's actually how geomorphologists describe the Sandhills, as fossil dunefields.

34 *pinpoint of star:* The reflection of the sun in every living thing's eyes.

with a splash: Figuratively splashing, not in the water but in the *place.* You arrive, and living things fly, swim, walk or run away and it takes awhile for the splash's ripples to die out, and fill back in around you. There are others, insects, that don't fit the metaphor. . . .

35 *pocket gophers:* These rodents live almost wholly underground, gnawing at roots and pulling stems down for eating and storage. In their burrowing they back the dirt up to the surface where it becomes an obvious sign of their presence. I think of them as nature's fallow, since the dirt mounds amount to that, and as the main inlets of the prairie soul, since the bare dirt in a monoculture of tame grasses, brome or crested wheatgrass say, is an opportunity for other plant species to go to seed.

rivers of air: On winter mornings one can go out and find, at certain cracks and holes in the earth, frost: the earth exhaled, here, there, last night. Where then does it inhale, and when? This viewpoint, subterranean, can wander the world as well as the aboveground view. It sees the hilltops warming first in the spring sun, almost glowing with heat, the vipers waking there. . .

Coyotes every night: Since April 26 I'd heard coyotes calling every night.

Where's the design: A little cowboy zen?

I resolve: I never did. Not in every watershed, that is.

37 *Even the hunter:* This is meant to counter any notions that hunters stupidly collide with their prey, and crassly kill it. Some do, but the essence of hunting is that to take a life you must first join it.

38 *A succession of generations:* See May 5 and 6.

rediscovering principles: Put it this way: are we doomed to repeat history whether or not we're paying attention?

39 *The absurd life:* Compare: the short life is an absurd one.

Page

41 *I don't get:* Overheard among thoughtful friends. The first statement was from a man from the eastern edge of the state, the reply was from a Rapid City resident.

42 *The trees are spilling:* Here we have a pocket history of trees on the Great Plains. It's possible the Plains were forested more than they are today during and after the glacial epochs, as the climate was cooler and wetter. A long drought in the 14th to 15th centuries may have finished them off, with only pockets of trees in sheltered, wet locations surviving. Now the Plains have millions of trees, either planted by people or protected from fire where they've grown naturally, as along the river valleys.

And oldest: Some of the rocks in the Black Hills have been dated at 2.5 billion years, some of the oldest exposed rock on earth.

The more they rise: Alternately, the more they river, the more they fall.

something exotic: Loons are fairly regular visitors to the Black Hills, (one per year) and otherwise are uncommon migrants in the rest of the state.

43 *birds still singing:* A situation that may have followed from the logging disturbances, not necessarily in spite of them.

one back home: Faulk County, east-river, where agriculture is the dominant land use.

44 The map is a tracing of a U.S. Forest Service map from the 1970's. Lead and Deadwood are evident near the north edge, Custer near the south edge. Some of these roads have been obliterated in the time since, while other new roads and trails have been built.

45 *In the Norbeck:* The Norbeck Wildlife Preserve, around Harney Peak and the Black Elk Wilderness, altogether one of the more roadless areas in the Hills. Now threatened by the Forest Service with an aggressive schedule of roadbuilding and logging.

without reaching for it: I'd stayed after my food ran out—it's so hard to leave—so I could have *used* that fish.

46 *the lowest full moon:* This long-period cycle of the moon's movement reached one extreme this year, with the full moon swinging low in the south by summer and high overhead in the winter. Also, the times between moonrises fluctuated greatly. They were over one hour apart from one night to the next in early June, but barely thirty minutes apart two weeks later. Nine years from now there will be less of a swing.

48 *lapse into Latin:* Another way words disappear: their roots you can travel down, like or as rain into the ground; follow the root and come back out as some other word—two words in a field full of them, their roots intertwined. Turf. Fruition is something else (publication?). May weeds disappear.

49 *flecked with gold:* Mostly mica, especially around Harney Peak, where the streams scintillate with the floating particles. They also hastened the plugging of my water filter.

spirit . . . breath: In that spirit is from the Latin word for breath, and that gradient is said to be the elixir of youth. (Which means the plains are the place to go to die?)

calamity's metal: Also called worrier's metal, gold is considered a safe investment in insecure times, such as war or threats of war. To invest in gold is to bet against your best wishes.

coins and jewelry: Some 60-70% of gold is used for jewelry and collectors' coins. What ivory is to elephants, gold is to the Black Hills. We're ripping the face off the earth to ornament ourselves.

49 *This is the feeling:* I may be overstating the situation, but I mean to suggest the enormity of what is current and potential for surface mining relative to the size of the Hills and to their long history, to see the mining as a major event even on a geologic time scale. That is, to start with the Hills' historic place and ecological preciousness and oppose that to the relatively sudden, profound, and permanent changes the mining imposes. And then ask what for? Jewelry? Especially set against the idea of the Hills as sacred, of any place as sacred, it becomes the ultimate in desecration, done to glorify ourselves.

The Black Hills are being assaulted on many fronts, public and private, but the gold mining is the ultimate aggression, tearing into a hillside to distill it into a few marble-sized bits of gold. It would cause less concern if the process wasn't potentially so toxic, if it wasn't for gold, to profit a few, if the Hills weren't so special, and being profoundly changed in the process.

Could it get worse? Oh, yes. Plans are being made to start a landfill just south of the Black Hills, for solid waste from other states. Importing trash at the south end and exporting gold from the north (because most of the gold comes from the northern Hills)—it sounds good, as if the one were being commuted to the other. But it's not going to happen that way, and is better expressed as exporting the riches of our state and importing trash.

have to decide: That's everybody's problem.

Page

50 *Indians to consecrate:* Refers to legislation in the U.S. Congress intended to return Federal lands in the Black Hills to the Sioux as reparation for treaty violations (the "Bradley Bill"). These lands were then to be used by the Sioux Nation in accordance with the principles of "respect for the earth."

1872. . . 1868: The Mining Law of 1872 gives preference to mineral extraction over all other uses of land; the Ft. Laramie Treaty of 1868 was intended to end hostilities between whites and the Sioux tribes. Among other provisions it set the boundaries of the Great Sioux Reserve—essentially what is now west-river South Dakota, plus parts of North Dakota, Wyoming, and Montana. Non-Indians were restricted in passing through the Reserve. While neither side adhered perfectly to the terms of the treaty, the pressure from white society to remove or exterminate the "heathen Indians" and settle the Plains was unmatched by any such dreams or attempts at empire or genocide on the part of Indians. In 1874 Gen. Custer led an expedition into the Black Hills, with two miners. Perhaps they knew if they found gold there would be no keeping people out. They did, and there was. In 1877 an act of Congress removed the Hills from within the boundaries of the Great Sioux Reserve.

belatedly declaring war: In the often emotional debate on the "Bradley Bill" a sentiment expressed by some white residents was that "we won the war, we've earned this land." Except that war was never officially declared. Which makes treaty violations all the more tragic: trickery during wartime is an expected practice, but during peacetime it's simply dishonorable.

cash as settlement: The U.S. Supreme Court in 1980 ruled in favor of the Sioux's claim to the Black Hills, filed in the U.S. Court of Claims in 1923. They were awarded $105 million as reparation, and have not accepted it. The award, with interest, has grown to over $200 million.

51 *planet joy:* Planet terror, more like, such as coasting down the "three-mile hills"—winding gravel roads going up and down the sides of a river valley—the steep gradient, curving road, loose rock surface, screaming brakes—

52 *a southeast-tending:* There is substantial literature that supports the idea that landforms are wind-shaped, including some subtle shaping of the relatively level plains (as compared with more vertical landforms that would be more exposed to the winds.) The mechanism responsible is usually thought to be wind-driven dust and ash during droughts and after fires. I think driven snow has been neglected in consideration as a mechanism, particularly for pushing the creeks draining the Hills (as Spring or Rapid Creeks) against the south side of their valleys.

Rain follows the plow: This was apparently a promotional phrase used to lure settlers from back East out to the plains. The hoax was in suggesting that plowing the prairie made it rain. It may have been meant to corrupt the Easterners' correct perception that farming here was risky because of scant rainfall.

55 *a yazoo stream:* A tributary that runs parallel to the larger river, essentially in the river valley, before emptying into the river.

56 *the rising sun:* Larger from shining through the morning haze of the James River valley. Going 150 miles northeast overnight meant entering that much farther into a wetter land, and more humid air. Here in the valley east is most always definitely not west. It's the difference between hazy dawn and dusty afternoon, although the distinction may be invisible at noon in July. Look closely at the eastern horizon and you can see that *it's all trees.* They're superimposed in a foreshortening of perspective, but some mornings the eastern land swings up into the sky in a mirage, and we can look among the farms and trees—it looks so inviting—with a view like the one available from these hills everyday. Look west and you can see clearly *between* the trees, which dribble out to ones and twos. Too clearly, and we peer between them a bit reluctantly: that way looks empty and endless. At night the farm lights confirm, and these all add up to a *feeling* of difference, that east will never be west here on these plains. The difference may be this definite over the length of the plains, as rain lays on the land in a striped pattern roughly aligned with the Rockies. Stripes of rain the sun crosshatches with light, that's life on the Great Plains. Settlers ply against them, and hang back to the east and to the south.

57 *all that is cold and flat:* This is for all those I've met not from here who shivered when I've said where I was from, or who croaked, "but it's so flat." Or who shivered and croaked both.

rebounding from the ice: The land beneath a glacier is depressed by the great mass, and slowly rebounds when the ice is gone. It is thought that Hudson Bay will no longer hold water once it completely rebounds.

(For an "understandable and uncomplicated" discussion of glaciers see *Living Ice* by Robert P. Sharp (Cambridge, 1988).)

59 *creeping and slow:* "Tire creep" is the term given to a tractor wheel's slipping back in trying to grip the ground and pull an implement forward.

61 *Our poor soils:* Because much of Iowa's deep topsoil consists of windblown sediments deposited over millions of years, much of it from glaciers and the rivers pouring therefrom. Without vegetation to hold

Page

it, the mud when it dried on the glaciers and riverbanks was free to roam southeast with the winds.

More than soil: The Missouri River flowing out the southeast corner drains virtually the whole state. The largest colleges and universities are—or were—concentrated in that corner, also.

62 *Easy food:* Easy is used two ways here: as "readily available" the first two times, and as "lazy" the third.

Drought years aside: Droughts and other widespread crop failures lead to higher crop prices but/because no one has much to sell.

63 *Still ringing:* One of the wettest years on record in South Dakota, 1986 left a legacy of healthy frog populations. Walking beside a marsh or creek in 1987 meant that a nearly continuous volley of frogs, mostly leopard frogs, was launched at my feet.

64 *I was there:* Here in the grass the whirlwinds are all but invisible, unless one passes nearby and the sound leads you to it. Other places in the valley, farmland, with the ground dug and bare, reveal the whirlwinds for miles around, sometimes in groups. Some are dark and well-defined columns, hollow and gently curved as pipestems blending earth and sky.

65 *that one word:* Smokies are a kind of sausage.

66 *it takes it out:* The second "it" refers to something like "spirit."

the poorer side: See page 53: "Topography is destiny."

67 *It's Thoreau:* Henry D. Thoreau apparently believed in reincarnation.

68 *the golden light:* See the last pages of Thoreau's essay, "Walking."

I come to the earth: This may be: a) high-flown language; b) some alien speaking through me; c) what the next three paragraphs are about; or d) about me. Raised on a great plain under dark night skies, reading science fiction—I've looked back at the earth. Space makes quibbling on earth obsolete as it makes earth precious: the unlimited raw materials of space are equaled by their lifelessness. In other words, there's no reason to fight, and this is no place to do it.

The other vision I have is that earth becomes one big airbase—level, paved, windswept. A spaceport. I've seen that future and turned from it; now at most it's a way to leave earth alone: to preserve it by leaving it.

And besides, the earth is a sitting duck for any dumb rock to collide with and *spoil everything*—we'd be wise to be mobile in space, and better our chances at survival. There'll be space stations for everybody, one for every allergen or (cynically) race to be avoided. And all the little space stations will probably sail around fighting and pirating. Eventually earth will be seen as too heavy a place—too hard to leave. "Anything drops to earth, forget it."

My point is that all those who would live space-station easy lives here now could just as well live in space, constructing their artificial environments there—the televised lives—unlimited—in space. Sterile air and fun. (You can still have houseplants.) These bio-engineered, robot-arm, electro-media, any-room-anywhere lives could be lived in space, and would you all please do just that, and soon? And leave the earth to us true canadians, before you turn it into a place that's space-station dead. Eventually we'll ignore you altogether, and receive not even, or especially, microwaves. If you have anything to report you may blink on and off, like a far-away planet in our night.

I'm sure I wouldn't want to live there, although I imagine you all wouldn't notice the difference, you wouldn't miss these cool green hills—

I know you would, that's when you would, when it was too late.

72 *if the fall is wet:* I should add: if the spring is wet.

73 *this V*: The hills east of the James River lead to or from a virtual point at their northern extreme. There was something of a split in the ice mantle here, with great lobes cruising south on either side. This map shows the feature well.

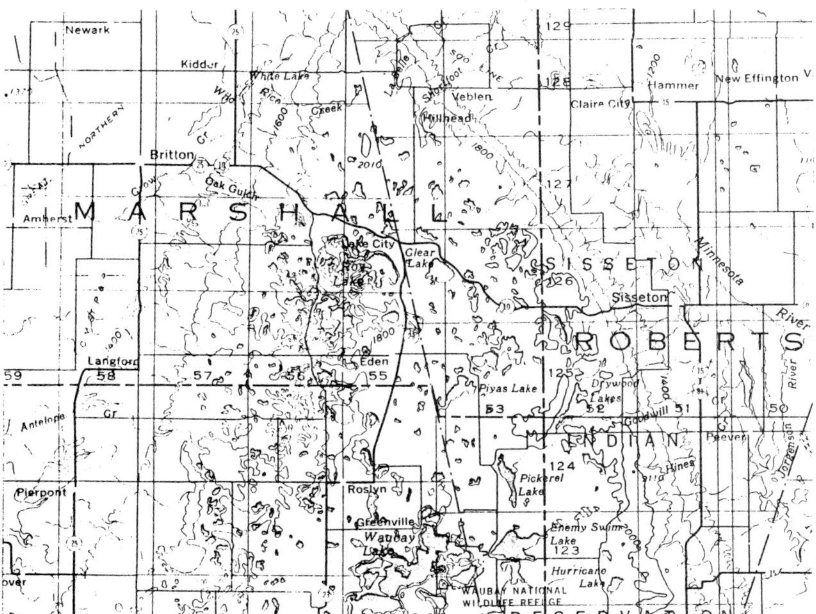

Page

76 *without losing track:* As when some fine series of thoughts comes along, I stop to record them, and they *stop.* And then if I learned to store them would I get lost in the stores and prefer them to new ones? Replay old ones under new guises? Can thoughts be guided without taming? Can they be untamed without going insane?

79 *against paper:* Or, casting the last tome.

80 *if pipit song:* You can substitute any local thing on this godsent earth that frees your heart as well as, I assure you, pipit song would.

earth. . . saved: When I composed this line this note was going to apologize for the phrasing. It was dated, and most of us had stopped using it for being too lofty, even impossible—the earth had better save us. After Earth Day, 1990 it came into overusage again. I should still apologize.

81 *like it that way:* For instance, see testimonials by Hans Oeschger, quoted in *Smithsonian*, May, 1989, p. 87; and Virginia I. Postrel in *Utne Reader*, July-August, 1990, p. 60-61. Or consider the statistic which claims that on average only 2% of our lives are spent outdoors.

82 *because they steal:* They say you can't eat scenery (before they excuse themselves for the work they do). They never say, "you can't eat TV's." And TV's ultimately eat scenery. . . .

difficult, dangerous: Not to mention citified and dangerous.

83 *blameless:* Yet I hardly take the stance that this is all innocent fun, or that I can just abandon these words on the world. I am wholly responsible for this book. At any time I could have set all this out for the wind to take away.

So long: I've found so many ways to say this I don't know where to end. If you can imagine, the last chapter was composed in a flourish some time ago as part of the first chapter, which made that one too long. Hatched whole, it now resists further revision and will have to stand on its own even as it cries out for elaboration, being too limited to a writer's role in the world's ecology and only hinting at what's worse.

Hypocrisy is a good place to begin. It goes to the heart, for expecting more (or less) from others than from myself is a charge that's been made to me more or less personally over the years in my role as environmentalist.* Do I really want a true ecological accounting of

*See, for instance, *The New Republic*, April 30, 1990, pp. 18-19 and pp. 31-32. A letter to the editor in the *Rapid City Journal* for Feb. 12, 1991, expresses this charge in typical fashion: "To all those who claim to be environmentalists—be an environmentalist 100 percent of the time regardless of the monetary cost to you, or get off the bandwagon."

everything I do, and would I follow its prescriptions? But those who charge me with hypocrisy seem to offer only a foolish kind of consistency in return: don't count the costs unless forced to, and then discount them. I recognize this urge in myself, but I don't let it rule me.

Consistency of belief and action is essential. Emptiness and frustration creep in when one or the other is ill. Belief is ideal and action imperfect, so my being imperfect is no excuse to dismiss my ideas. They, not my performance, are what's being offered here for trial. At least I'm trying to weigh the costs, and lessen my part. At least I'm setting a direction and heading along it. Worse hypocrisy would be having these ideas and not acting on them. Worse yet would be not caring.

I recognize myself in all of this. My own transgressions are the most painful, sickening me at times while at others I join in freely. I want more than I need. I spoil myself. I eat badly, or use food for solace. I watch, I drive, I drink, I waste, I'm crass, I'm nobody special, I do my share. I add up. But I've set a direction and can measure my progress by looking back to see how I've subtracted, to see some way of doing or thinking that I've outgrown, or something I once needed but now do without. I'm regularly abashed by the memories, some of them recent, to see how I once behaved. So I'm as hard on myself as anyone else would be, which leads to the question: if I think I'm not conscientious enough, where behind me are those who couldn't care less?

All my choices and all I do, as much as they are is as much as I am responsible for, as much as I can subtract. My part's a pittance, but only to scale. In principle my part's exemplary: *what if everyone did this?*

'Environmentalist' is more than a role that some of us play. If we don't lead by example, who will? For instance, if living simply is a direction we would set, because we would take no more than necessary from the earth, we should lead that way gladly if it means that much to us. If we really love the earth we'd be out in it, being the least we can be to it and from it: *only cast shadow.* But withdrawing to an earthly asceticism would hardly communicate. So we feel the tensions in being a part of a system we're trying to change, in subtracting ourselves while reaching to include others, and we lead double lives, many of us—as bridges will.

The example we should set, I think, is a society that lives lightly on the earth, lightly and well, asking the least of the earth to preserve it as home. It is starting point and direction and possibly an end: living light may mean living well, by needing the least from the world to be thriving and happy. It's just a challenge, no cause for alarm, a question of design, a direction to set; what else is there to do? How can we eat without losing soil? Without needing to kill? How do we keep warm in winter and cool in summer? How can we move from place to place? How can we live without needing as much?

A true accounting that misses nothing is called for. It attempts the most honest and all-embracing view of a situation. At its purest it is simple: everything we do is ecological. We can't take a breath or utter a word and think that's the end of it. The smallest gesture can reverberate and return, amplified. No island is an island, and none is too small to be significant. Footprints count. Even play can be serious: dance too long in one place and you kill the grass. (Pave it, then.) Learn how the least of your being, your shadow, takes from the world and gives to it.

We create conditions we'll have to respond to, then we'll have to respond to our responses. Who can keep track of it? It's complicated, but fairly to a degree that one's life is. To simplify one's life is to simplify the process of understanding it and its effects. It's easier to count if there's less to count. (But you can't squirm out of this by counting less than what you're responsible for—that's the first hypocrisy.) Light living occurs, as well as any direction in life that requires fewer costs and less counting.

The life of a nomad that I virtually leapt to in 1987 obliges this simplicity, needing less for having less for carrying only so much. There are steps down in material, but these are rewarded and replaced by other satisfactions: landscapes, the play of light and cloud, birdsong and stars. . .this free spectacular scene. Time is freed to enjoy the splendor, not lost earning excess baggage. Traveling light means less fat on your muscles; less fat means you are well in body. (Then behold your vision becoming centered, spherical, in a circular church that is ever with you. No windows. Light from all sides. The ceremony is whatever the weather is. Where are the thunder buttes? The eagle buttes? Medicine knolls?)

Nomadism required and enhanced the deep connection with the land that I set out to celebrate. It was immersion and immediacy, for a connection abetted by clearing away what gets in the way: the props, the media, eventually even the self: giving myself to these places to learn their language and speak for them. It won't allow accumulation, which comes at too high a price: the loss of connection.

Whether it's lived as a nomad or settler, the relationship is personal and memorable and not so strained by distance your effects seem unimportant to you or the world around you. You can see firsthand how your needs can lessen the world that gives them meaning.

It's hard not to take from the earth, hard to know when you're taking too much. It's a restless dialogue between what I need and what the world allows: whether to form or conform? It's especially hard to count the costs when the effects come so late or diluted we can't recognize or feel them. Or when the costs appear only in the aggregate, by adding up—all of us living here as we do. (Living here is the part that won't change soon.)

The fact of my ecological significance is deeply masked by its scale. Meaning seems to give out early in the measurement. My efforts are puny and my effects miniscule; it's hard enough to care without feeling small. This is my first and last chance to escape responsibility, by denying my own meaning. Instead I set out to give my life meaning at least by measuring it. Soon, very soon, scale becomes the whole point, and the mind for its size appears as the richest matter around, being here mostly and exquisitely without intruding, embracing so much terrain with so little energy. Thought is the most and lightest life, and travel. But I hope I don't go too far, to thinking my shadow is too much, or even more than me.

Without intruding, without dissolving: around here if you only cast shadow long enough you'll be nibbled to nothing by crickets. Well, nobody claimed this would be easy. Learning to live simply and well anywhere on this inconstant planet is a task as long as life itself. The earth never was a free ride, but some of us seem to have overcompensated for the fact. We've come so far beyond basic needs we've forgotten what it means to satisfy them. We've come so far it may take a leap back, past all the belongings that hide the meaning for us to rediscover that meaning, in having water to drink, shelter from rain, light into the night. (Floods and hurricanes and earthquakes force this leap.) Instead we reach a level and accustom to it. Soon it's not good enough and we want more. Then we attain that and immediately want more. And over the years and generations we forget how we could live without some things, much more what it means to have riches. Our wants extend so far beyond need we're more needy than ever. How did we get to be like this, in lives of need despite our riches?

Who can remember or reconstruct what it was like to be alive on the Plains a hundred or more years ago? To be a person native, waking to another morning, what that person knew and expected, what the world was like then— To be able to raise a tent was a step up, but also a step down, by separation. In the time since, separation has become the custom, but did people back then want to rise as far from the earth as we've made our habit?

We are few of us earthly people anymore. Who among us lives so intimately with a place that we earn it, as much as possession is, by our presence, attention, and memory? Along the way we lost sight of what a joy the earth can be, and that beyond our needs is the time to enter that joy. When our riches reach a certain level we have the ability to go without, by choice. (Much of the world doesn't share this.) Is it possible to live today with a 20th century style at an 18th century pace?

Instead our direction is to ignore how our needs take from the world, and how our wants beyond necessity steal even more. We internalize costs to ourselves while recklessly externalizing costs to the earth. We exist in the world ecologically—there's no escape—without knowing it or acknowledging it. And every step in that direction is one we'll have to give back someday.

There is some failure in needing, especially more than we really need. We know it secretly and disguise it as ability: we keep multiplying our needs, and because some of us can meet those needs we define that as success. The fact that we need more than people did one hundred years ago is ignored; it would undermine our notions of progress.

Somewhere along the line we replaced the idea of progress with the idea of growth, until now many of our measurements measure gross, unsophisticated, omnidirectional growth regardless of quality. Are we stuck in an economist's dream? People go so far in describing and defining their lives in economic terms they forget how it could be otherwise. They play along, and call it work. They learn to like it, and define personal growth as merely additive growth, as accumulation, wealth, influence, offspring. Become as easy in wasting as in wanting more. Don't count the costs, or figure them later. In the cities they pave the ground—not for dancing—and stack themselves, ever more a teeming whole even as they protest, mumbling, to it for being crowded, lonely, frantic, anonymous, empty, absurd. Ever more plugging into it, depending on it, lost in it. Unable to feed or clothe or house themselves they reach impersonally and almost bodilessly by roads and pipelines beyond their limits to the country for sustenance and to wilderness for energy and materials. Always discounting the cost. Disconnected and unconcerned, they like it that way and want to keep it that way, trifling and relinquishing what makes them human while humanizing machines. They perceive true ecological reckoning as a threat to their way of life, and maybe they're right. Maybe they do have it too well, comfort enough for ten lifetimes and nine are stolen. In the process whole landscapes of the earth are being consumed, land and sea converted by money into more money. The future looks ever-more artificial, ultimately like a space station: the earth as so much sunlit and windswept real estate. And beyond this there are planets galore to waste, if you can get to them.

If that's how it is to be then the future is up for grabs, to whomever gets there first. It's your word against mine, and I'm going to stand for every voiceless place on earth that I can to keep it from you—